FOUR
IN THE EARLY CHURCH

ROD BENNETT

FOUR MORE WITNESSES IN THE EARLY CHURCH

Further Testimony from
Christians before Constantine

IGNATIUS PRESS   SAN FRANCISCO

Cover art and design by
Christopher J. Pelicano

© 2021 by Ignatius Press, San Francisco
All rights reserved
ISBN 978-1-62164-374-6 (PB)
ISBN 978-1-64229-170-4 (eBook)
Library of Congress Control Number 2021932658
Printed in the United States of America ∞

This book is gratefully dedicated to the memory of

Clive Staples Lewis

Who first set me looking for that Church
"spread through all time and space and rooted
in eternity, terrible as an army with banners".

Complete my joy by being of the same mind, having the same love, being in full accord and of one mind.

—Philippians 2:2

Contents

Introduction

Welcome back!

It has been my great privilege for almost twenty years now to see the original *Four Witnesses* become so helpful to so many. If discovering the existence of authentic writings from Christianity's "second generation" of saints marked a revolution in my own journey, I have watched that revolution enacted many times since in the reports I continue to receive from readers of all different faith backgrounds, from all over the world. My prayer at the time of that initial publication has certainly been answered: "May the Holy Spirit use this new book to kindle in your hearts—as He has in mine—a bit of the fire and passion of your spiritual ancestors as they write to us from across the centuries *in their own words*."

Some of those readers have felt passionate enough to wonder whether there might not be *more* such stories remaining to be told; and this new volume does contain four more, about characters whose lives and teachings are, I think, equally instructive. Hermas, as you will see, was the contemporary of Clement of Rome, who acted as the first of what are now *eight* witnesses, all told. Clement of Alexandria, second in this volume, was a disciple of Irenaeus, our final witness from the original book. Hippolytus and Origen were both disciples of Clement of Alexandria. So once again, the "chain of custody" for the teachings being passed on reaches backward into the age of the Apostles, just as it did with their predecessors. The narrative contained in this second book concludes in the year A.D. 253—still six decades before the conversion of Constantine.

There seems less need for an extended introduction this time around. In fact, I ought to go ahead and warn any late-comers to the party that I have not taken up any time or space in these pages at all for a recap of the first book. I will not say that *Four More Witnesses* will leave you *completely* in the dark if you have not looked at the original—only that I have taken your awareness of the points established in Book One completely for granted here, so heads up.

Alas, not quite everyone was enthusiastic about *Four Witnesses*—and a certain subset of those negative comments bears mentioning here. As soon as the book was published in 2002, I began to notice that a really surprising number of readers took the trouble to report that they had devoured the book avidly and were loving what they read . . . until they got to the afterword at the end, where, totally out of the blue, the author dragged in the "Roman Catholic Church", of all preposterous things. One might have supposed that, for careful readers like these, the trouble I took to establish that these early Fathers accepted regenerating infant baptism, authoritative bishops and priests, a sacrificial Lord's Supper, and a special role for the bishop of Rome as successor of St. Peter might have acted as a canary in that particular coal mine well before page 281; but let us judge not that we be not judged.

Having said this, however, I would like to reassert something I believe I did express in that very same afterword: the fact, that is, that I never actually insisted all of my readers *must* reach precisely my own conclusions on the topic at hand. I was offering a personal testimony in that portion of the book, a piece of shameless autobiography dealing entirely with my own reaction to discovering the Fathers. "Yes," I wrote, "'High Church' Episcopalians do claim to be able to find their religion in the writings of our four witnesses. And yes, the Eastern [Orthodox] churches do venerate these very writings, . . . insisting that theirs is the faith revealed in those pages." And, as a matter of fact, both of those great communions really are historically rooted in the very same undivided ante-Nicene Church we visited in *Four Witnesses*. "Except", as I have written elsewhere, "for a few final vexing questions among these churches (almost all of which deal with issues of polity and governance, the least urgent matters, surely, for laypeople), these three great bodies are undivided still", retaining, as they do, the recognizable faith of the early Fathers even now in their official creeds and confessions. And though I do retain my own definite opinion about where the buck finally does stop in those ultimate issues of Church government, I am still not trying to get everyone across the finish line in this particular book (or pair of books). I am not, of course, retracting the wholehearted apologia for the Roman claims I offered at the conclusion of *Four Witnesses*; I willingly confess that on that score "I would that all men were even as I myself." But if I could believe I had gotten my readership ninety-five miles down the road in a one-hundred-mile journey, I would feel confident, I think, in leaving the last five miles to their own investigations, standing within sight of just three or four large, well-used doors—and be pleased to consider it a good twenty-years' work.

I will be frank, though. The ninety-five-mile journey will have ruled out anything like modern American Evangelicalism in the end (as you probably realized after completing

Four Witnesses). Happily, many of its best ideas and instincts were hold-overs from the movement's catholic and liturgical origins anyway, which inquirers may not only retain at the conclusion of journeys like this one but will find gratefully and unreservedly seconded. Yet the need to accomplish the exodus is urgent. Denominational Christianity is visibly failing, and should fail, based as it is on false history —in a religion that is, of all religions, the most historical. The only real question now is: Can it fail without leaving its now-familiar trail of cynical and embittered "Nones" in its wake? "It [denominationalism] is the form that religion takes in a culture controlled by the ideology of the Enlightenment" wrote Anglican bishop Lesslie Newbigin. "It is the social form in which the privatization of religion is expressed. . . . It follows that neither a denomination separately nor all the denominations linked together in some kind of federal unity or 'reconciled diversity' can be the agents of a missionary confrontation with our culture, for the simple reason that they are themselves the outward and visible signs of an inward and spiritual surrender to the ideology of our culture. They cannot confront our culture with the witness of the truth since even for themselves they do not claim to be more than associations of individuals who share the same private opinions."[1]

The Fathers show the way out.

The quest to spread the word that *"The early Church is no mystery"* is a movement for Christian unity.

---

[1] Lesslie Newbigin, *Foolishness to the Greeks: The Gospel and Western Culture* (Grand Rapids, Mich.: Eerdmans, 1986, pp. 145–46).

A Note about Terminology

All three of the great Christian traditions to which I alluded in my introduction—the Western or Roman Catholic Church, the Eastern Orthodox Churches, and the worldwide Anglican communion—still employ the term "Catholic" to refer to the original, apostolic faith described in the writings of the early Fathers, which is also the sense in which I will be using it here.

All three of those traditions also use the word "saint" in a manner that may be unfamiliar or questionable to those from an Evangelical background. While agreeing that *all* of the faithful are termed "saints" in the New Testament, the ancient churches apply that title more specially to those saints now reigning with Christ in heaven and whose lives (after being carefully examined by ecclesiastical authority) have been judged worthy of honors and emulation by those of us still on earth. The early records (some of which will be examined in this book) show that the intercession of such glorified saints has been invoked during the common Eucharistic Prayers since at least the second century.

Finally, the title of "pope" (derived from the Greek word *papas*, an affectionate diminutive for *Father*) was, up until the mid-fifth century, used Church-wide to address any important patriarch of the Catholic Church, not just the bishop of Rome; i.e., Athanasius became "pope of Alexandria", John Chrysostom was "pope of Constantinople", and so forth. That is the sense in which I will be using it in these pages,

without insisting on any of the disputed Roman preroga-
tives (though, as a coincidental matter of fact, all the clerics
to whom I have applied the title here do happen to have
been bishops of Rome).

Abbreviations

ACW   Ancient Christian Writers Series. Mahwah, N.J.,
      Paulist Press.

ANF   *Ante-Nicene Fathers*, edited by Alexander Roberts
       and James Donaldson, revised by A. Cleveland Coxe.
       Peabody, Mass.: Hendrickson Publishers, 1995.

CE   *The Catholic Encyclopedia*, found online at: newad
      vent.org/cathen/

FEF   *The Faith of the Early Fathers*, translated and edited
       by W. A. Jurgens, 3 vols. Collegeville, Minn.: Litur-
       gical Press, 1970–1979.

Hermas and His Shepherd

Anybody could be a Church Father—even Joe Schmoe.

Clement of Rome is mentioned in the Bible and eventually became bishop of the Church "founded and organized at Rome by the two most glorious Apostles, Peter and Paul".[1] Ignatius was Peter's successor at Antioch, the church where disciples of Christ were first called "Christians".[2] Justin Martyr had been a layperson, to be sure, but a very unusual one—the greatest theologian of his age. And Irenaeus of Lyons, the Church's early expert against all heresies, had been discipled by the great martyr Polycarp.

But Hermas? Hermas was nobody—the nobody of the nobodies. To begin with, he was born into slavery; or perhaps he was picked up by slave traders off the *spurci lacus*, the blood-stained piazza in Rome where unwanted infants were left to die. If so, he had likely been the product of adultery or some other kind of illicit union; the poet Ovid, for instance, writes of the exposure of Canace's baby son, born of the incest she committed with her brother, a child whose own grandfather had ordered thrown to the wild dogs and carrion birds. Either way, Hermas lacked what they used to call *good breeding* . . . to say the least. And he grew up

---

[1] Irenaeus of Lyons, *Against Heresies*, bk. 3, chap. 3, no. 2, in *The Faith of the Early Fathers*, trans. and ed. W. A. Jurgens (hereafter abbreviated *FEF*), vol. 1 (Collegeville, Minn.: Liturgical Press, 1970), p. 90, no. 210.

[2] Cf. Acts 11:26.

to young adulthood as a human chattel, pure and simple, a living farm implement picking vegetables under the hot Italian sun on a big plantation located on the main highway between Rome and Cumae. Hermas never became a presbyter, a bishop, an apologist, or even, as far as we know, a martyr or confessor. He did become a Christian, of course, probably when his original owner sold him to a Christian lady named Rhoda, not much older than he. But even Hermas himself frankly confesses that his early observance was rote and perfunctory.[3] Rhoda seems to have given him some elementary instruction, had him baptized, and then put him to work—much as Christian slaveholders in the Old South were usually careful to do with their own "property".[4]

Okay, then, this must be another story about a great saint with humble beginnings—right? Alas, not so much. Hermas earned his place among the Church Fathers by the writing of just one book; and even that one provides am-

---

[3] That rote observance may seem odd coming so near to the age of the Apostles. Mere perfunctory compliance seems always to have been an option in the Church, especially for those of us born into Christian homes without the benefit of some dramatic adult conversion experience or otherwise grandfathered-in—like Hermas.

[4] The Apostles and earliest Fathers did not attack the institution of slavery directly; their influence in the political sphere was, in these early centuries, too negligible to make cries for legal change anything but laughable. What they did do was to attack, simply by preaching the authentic Catholic message, the underlying pagan assumptions that made slavery thinkable; as, for instance, St. Paul's radical assertion that in the Church "there is neither Jew nor Greek, there is neither slave nor free, there is neither male nor female; for you are all one in Christ Jesus" (Gal 3:28). As European society became more and more contiguous with Christianity itself and thus gradually infused with this higher conception, slavery died a slow, natural death—until revived during the Renaissance by the return of a skeptical, quasi-pagan "humanism".

ple evidence of its author's many shortcomings. Unlike his great contemporary Justin, for instance, who, after his conversion from paganism, learned an astonishing amount of Scripture in a very short time and employed that knowledge skillfully throughout his works, Hermas' book contains not one single Bible quotation, only a few allusions and a loose paraphrase or two. So our subject had, it seems, like so many of us, heard a lot of Scripture read in church and tried to incorporate what he had heard into his own talk—but could not give you chapter and verse and seldom attempted a real quote for fear of fouling it up in front of people.[5] And quite unlike Irenaeus, a master of Christian divinity (as that science stood, at least, about the year 180), Hermas' theology was nothing to wire home about, either. In fact, it is downright wonky in spots; not actually heretical, mind you, just not cobbled together exactly right.[6] Hermas made a mess of his family life as well. Freed, as we shall see, by his mistress Rhoda and set up with a small plot of his own to farm, manumission proved no real blessing to our protagonist. Hermas, by his own account, became so preoccupied with making a go of it, so entangled in what our

---

[5] Actually, the earliest divisions of the biblical books into chapters were not made until the ninth century; and French Calvinist Robert Estienne created the verse divisions in the 1550s.

[6] "It has been thought with some reason that he did not distinguish the Son from the Holy Ghost, or that he held that the Holy Ghost became the Son by His Incarnation. But his words are not clear, and his ideas on the subject may have been rather misty and confused than definitely erroneous." (Article on "Hermas" in the *Catholic Encyclopedia* (hereafter abbreviated *CE*), found online at www.newadvent.org/cathen/07268b.htm). Hermas wrote, after all, about two hundred years before the carefully thought out definitions of the First Council of Nicaea were drawn up.

Lord called "the cares of the world",[7] that he neglected his wife to the point of estrangement and spoiled his children so badly that they apostatized the first chance they got and reverted to the life-style of the surrounding paganism. And then the farm failed anyway.

Yet for all of this, Hermas' *Shepherd* is probably the single noncanonical Christian book that came closest to making the final cut as Scripture. Irenaeus, in fact, calls it Scripture in so many words; and Codex Sinaiticus, one of the three or four oldest Bibles in the world, includes *The Shepherd* as part of its New Testament. Codex Claromontanus, another early Bible, slips it in right after *The Acts of the Apostles*. Indeed, the book was so widely circulated during the second and third centuries that there are actually more surviving manuscripts of *The Shepherd* in existence than of several canonical books! The great Athanasius continued to recommend it and to quote from it even after its shaky Christology became useful to the Arian party—and the more you learn about Athanasius and his attitude toward Arianism, the more significant this fact becomes.[8]

How did this happen? How did Joe Schmoe get this close to having his name enshrined forever alongside Peter and Paul, Matthew, Mark, Luke, and John? Certainly, Hermas himself attempted no fraud; he simply wrote down his own account of a series of dreams he experienced and submitted

---

[7] Mk 4:19. All Bible quotations are, unless otherwise noted, taken from the Revised Standard Version, Second Catholic Edition.

[8] Those interested in learning more about St. Athanasius and the great Arian crisis of the fourth century might enjoy a look at one of this author's previous works, *The Apostasy that Wasn't: The Extraordinary Story of the Unbreakable Early Church* from Catholic Answers Press.

them humbly to his pastor. He would, we feel sure, have been as surprised as anyone to see his name listed alongside these pillars of the faith. We would like to be able to say that reading *The Shepherd* for yourself would solve the mystery; that Hermas' book is so uplifting, so obviously "inspired" in the colloquial sense, that one can easily see how early Christian leaders might have found themselves compelled to believe they were encountering sacred writ. But the truth is that *The Shepherd* is a pretty odd piece of work; the autobiographical portions have a certain rural charm, but the rest reads like a rather strained and at times confusing imitation of the book of Revelation crossed with something like *Pilgrim's Progress*. There are, at any rate, at least a half-dozen other works more or less contemporary with *The Shepherd* that "sound" on the face of things much more like something one might find in the Bible: documents like the *Letters of Ignatius*, the *Epistle to Diognetus*, the *Epistle of Barnabas*, or even the *Martyrdom of Polycarp*. Why, then, did *The Shepherd* seem so important to so many of the great minds of Christian antiquity? What caused Eusebius of Caesarea to report—nearly two hundred years after its composition —that Hermas' curious little phantasmagoria was still being read liturgically from the pulpit in many places and that numerous great elders of the Church "considered it most necessary"?[9]

Though it is not the easiest narrative in the world of which to make heads or tails, the story of how Hermas the no-account, Hermas the bankrupt, Hermas who never did

---

[9] Eusebius, quoted in the article on "Hermas", in *CE*, found online at www.newadvent.org/cathen/07268b.htm.

get his family back or his farm as far as we know, came so close to literary immortality while still managing to finish up as a footnote and an also-ran is well worth taking the trouble to master. While it was certainly a mistake to try and mark it as the written Word of God, thinking long and hard about *The Shepherd* and the issues it raised really does seem to have been uniquely helpful in the quest to recognize the final, correct list of Christian Scriptures as we have it today. Even more important, however, is the actual content of the writing. *The Shepherd* is, at heart, a book about *baptism*: what it is, what it does . . . and what it *does not* do. And it rose to prominence during a period when the baptismal doctrine expressed in the book began to be challenged for the first time—and challenged, eventually, from a stunningly unexpected quarter. This being the case, plain old Hermas has, in spite of everything, provided us with critical, even *decisive* evidence for settling several of the most important debates still dividing Evangelicalism from more traditional forms of Christianity.

The Pastor's Package

In the modern city of Rome, not much more than a stone's throw from the Coliseum, visitors may find the beautiful Basilica di San Clemente al Laterano, the most recent of three Christian churches that have stood on the same spot since the days of the early Fathers. Recent is, of course, a relative term when it comes to Roman buildings; construction on this existing edifice commenced under the auspices of Pope Paschal II about the turn of the twelfth century. Paschal commissioned the new San Clemente to replace the earlier basilica of that name in which he himself had been

consecrated, a church burned to its foundations in 1084 by
the invading Normans under Robert Guiscard. That building—the second tier of our three-layer cake, so to speak
—had been, to Paschal, only modestly more "recent" than
the one we have today. Ordered up by the newly converted
Emperor Constantine about 750 years prior to Paschal's
era, it too served as a replacement for an earlier church,
the really ancient church at the bottom of the stack uncovered by archaeologists in 1914. Though it had been buried
more than seventeen centuries by that time, the Christians
of Rome were not surprised by its discovery, for they had
always remembered that it was there, a hidden source of the
site's immemorial identification with St. Clement I, bishop
of Rome in the 90s A.D. and third successor to the chair
of Peter. And, yes, St. Clement, as readers of *Four Witnesses*
have likely realized by now, is that self-same Clement of
Rome whom we first met in those pages.

How did we get back around to Clement in a chapter
that is supposed to be about Hermas? Well, Hermas, if one
looks carefully, turns up as the central character of an *untold
subplot* in the story of Clement's career; a subplot that likely
began with the delivery of an unexpected package to his office here at the original San Clemente (whatever a "church
office" may have looked like during the final decade of that
amazing century that began at Bethlehem).[10] The package

---

[10] Architecturally speaking, Clement's church is not a church at all but
only a fairly typical villa house that appears once to have belonged to a Roman nobleman. It may be that this nobleman, whoever he was—perhaps
a converted magistrate or a retired military officer—offered his home for
use as a house church to replace earlier meeting places destroyed during
the Great Fire of 64 (other ruins nearby show signs of the damage).

probably contained a box, and the box a scroll made from many papyrus sheets pasted end to end—a book, in other words, as books existed in those days. Along with the scroll, there was, more than likely, a cover letter as well; and from this letter Clement would have learned that the book had been composed by a member of his own Roman flock—a freedman named Hermas—and that the making of it had been ordered by an angel (or so said its author). And the angel, supposedly, had singled out Clement by name and directed that this particular manuscript be created specifically for him.

Cranks and screwballs, like the poor, we shall doubtless always have with us—and there is no reason to think that a seasoned first-century pastor had seen fewer than we do nowadays or been any more susceptible to their delusions. In fact, Clement's first inclination may very well have been to consign Hermas' *Shepherd* unceremoniously to the bin. Why did he not do so? It is highly unlikely that Clement had any personal knowledge of Hermas, of the type that might have earned him a reading. Rome was the largest city on earth at that time, with a population reliably estimated at 400,000 to 500,000 souls. Additional estimates suggest that there were at least 50,000 Christians in the empire by the year 100, probably half of whom lived at Rome. This being the case, Clement was almost certainly a metropolitan bishop already in something like our modern sense: general overseer of multiple local congregations spread city-wide and not just of his own church there on the Via Labicana —leaving Hermas one more sheep, really, in a very large flock. Nor would a casual perusal of the first few pages have grabbed the bishop's attention in any of the ordinary ways. As one might expect of a farmer, Hermas' Greek composition is terrible: "His grammar is faulty, his style clumsy and diffuse, and filled with long sentences and wearisome repetitions . . . his logic is extremely defective; he does not even know the art of writing correctly."[11] Clement would have quickly detected all the other faults we have noted as well: the lack of a strong scriptural foundation, the dicey theology, and the rest. And yet he did read the book; and what is more, he did ultimately send it out with his approval to "make the rounds" of the other churches[12]—just as Hermas' angel had instructed: "**[This vision, Hermas] will be made known to all the elect through you. Therefore you will write two little books, and you will send one to Clement and one to Grapte. Then Clement will send it to the cities abroad, because that is his job. But Grapte will instruct the widows and orphans.**[13] **But you yourself will read it to this city, along with the elders who preside over the church.**"[14]

What was it about that first perusal which drew the bishop in, despite everything? What overcame the instinct for

---

[11] J. Tixeront, *Handbook of Patrology*, quoting A. Lelong, in *Textes et Documents: Les Pères Apostoliques*, vol. 3, *Ignace d'Antioche* (Paris, 1910), found online at: www.earlychristianwritings.com/tixeront/section1-1.html#hermas.

[12] The Latin word *encyclius*—adapted from the Greek *enkyklios*, meaning "circular" or "in a circle"—came to be used by the early Church to describe an epistle sent out by a bishop to be read aloud in all the parishes of his diocese. These days a "papal encyclical" is any letter issued by the pope of Rome as a message intended for the whole Church.

[13] Grapte is a woman's name; she was probably a deaconess at the Roman Church, of the type St. Paul mentions in Romans 16:1 when commending "our sister Phoebe".

[14] Unless otherwise noted, all quotations from *The Shepherd of Hermas* are taken from *The Apostolic Fathers in English*, trans. Michael W. Holmes, 3rd ed. (Grand Rapids, Mich.: Baker Academic, 2007). Here, 2.4, no. 8, p. 211.

skepticism? Probably it was the character of Hermas himself, as he reveals it while telling his own backstory; Hermas, as others besides Clement have concluded, just comes off as a nice guy. "Although not a learned man, he is a shrewd observer and has a sane and just mind, a tender heart, and good practical judgment. . . . He is very considerate and moderate . . . and, in consequence of the deep sense he has of divine mercy, shows himself very lenient and optimistic."[15] Hermas' heavenly visitors noticed the same qualities, and he innocently records their reasons for choosing him as the recipient of their revelations without any effort at false modesty: " '[a man] patient and good-natured, always laughing', 'full of all sincerity and of great innocence' ".[16] "Hermas", as another writer concludes, "depicts himself as slow of understanding but insatiable in curiosity, . . . a simple man of limited outlook, but genuinely pious and conscientious".[17] These are not the qualities that experienced clergymen have learned to expect from nuts and oddballs, the sort of people who usually show up at church claiming to have heard from angels. In brief, the presence of *humility* in a visionary or modern-day prophet sets off alarm bells . . . of the good kind.

Certainly, Clement would not have dismissed the very idea that God might speak to a lowly working man in a dream; he had, after all, known at least one such man personally, whose dreams, to say the least, came with the most unimpeachable authenticity—we mean, of course, the blessed Apostle Peter. The Big Fisherman "fell into a trance",

---

[15] Joseph Tixeront, *A Handbook of Patrology*.

[16] *Shepherd of Hermas*, 1.2, *Apostolic Fathers*, p. 207.

[17] Bruce Metzger, *The Canon of the New Testament: Its Origin, Development, and Significance* (Oxford: Clarendon Press, 1997), p. 65.

we are told in Acts 10:10, during which God revealed the
momentous vision that had opened the door of faith to a
Gentile like Clement in the first place: the image of the great
linen sheet descending from heaven, filled with animals both
clean and unclean. Paul, too, had seen an angel during the
night (Acts 27:23) and elsewhere reports that while "praying
in the temple, I fell into a trance" and saw Jesus deliver a
warning to leave Jerusalem (Acts 22:17–18). Paul definitely
accepted, as well, that such things might happen to laypeople as much as to Apostles; nearly a whole chapter of his
First Epistle to the Corinthians is devoted to assessing and
regulating that very phenomenon: "Make love your aim,
and earnestly desire the spiritual gifts, especially that you
may prophesy. . . . He who prophesies speaks to men for
their upbuilding and encouragement and consolation. . . .
He who prophesies edifies the Church. . . . So, my brethren,
earnestly desire to prophesy, . . . but all things should be
done decently and in order" (1 Cor 14:1, 3, 4b, 39, 40). This
last phrase, of course, shows the Apostle was not unaware of
the inherent risks in such a broad welcome. He was surely
familiar, in fact, with the well-known warning about such
things in the book of Sirach: ". . . dreams are folly, and . . .
the mind has fancies. Unless they are sent from the Most
High as a visitation, do not give your mind to them. For
dreams have deceived many, and those who put their hope
in them have failed" (Sir 34:5–7).[18] Even so, it had been

---

[18] Written about 180 B.C., the book of Sirach was widely studied by
knowledgeable Jews like Paul and accepted as part of the Word of God
by most (at least throughout the first century). St. Paul's epistles to the
Romans and Ephesians seem to contain brief allusions to it, while the
("Pauline" in some sense) book of Hebrews adopts Sirach's "Heroes Hall
of Fame" listing practically wholesale (Heb 11).

Peter himself who boldly linked the words of the prophet Joel to the new state of affairs revealed at Pentecost: "I will pour out my Spirit upon all flesh, and your sons and your daughters shall prophesy, and your young men shall see visions, and your old men shall dream dreams" (Acts 2:17). And Paul doubled down, in First Thessalonians, on both the warning and the welcome: "Do not quench the Spirit, do not despise prophesying, but test everything; hold fast what is good" (5:19–21).

"Do not despise prophesying." This, perhaps, was the word that stayed Clement's hand as it hovered over the wastebasket—personal disciple, as he was, of both Peter and Paul. Moreover, there was just something about *The Shepherd* itself that seemed . . . timely. Uncannily so, in fact. Yes, Hermas relates his own personal testimony in the book—of a just-in-time escape from lukewarm nominalism made possible by a supernatural shock to the system—but to a conscientious shepherd of souls like Clement, the story must have read like a heavenly wake-up call for an entire generation.

Contrary to popular belief, persecution of Christians was not constant or widespread during the first century. After Nero's psychotic rampage of A.D. 64, it was many years before another general persecution broke out; and the fact that the public had difficulty distinguishing Christians from Jews early on (as most of them still were, ethnically or at least culturally) allowed believers to take advantage of the same legal concessions that traditional Jews had carved out for themselves over the past century or so.[19] This peace was,

---

[19] "Writing around [A.D.] 90, the Jewish author Josephus cited decrees by Julius Caesar, Mark Antony, Augustus and Claudius, granting Jewish communities with a number of rights." Wikipedia: wikipedia.org/wiki/History _of_the_Jews_in_the_Roman_Empire#cite_note-6.

however, a double-edged sword when it came to the health of the Church. That generation that had, in the earliest days of Gospel preaching, "laid down their burdens, down by the riverside" and rejoiced afterward to cry out with David, "Bless the LORD, O my soul, . . . who forgives all your iniquity, . . . who redeems your life from the Pit,"[20] had now grown old and was passing away. And as the Bridegroom tarried ten, twenty, fifty years or more, many of their children and grandchildren, like the ten foolish virgins, now "slumbered and slept".[21]

If, as we believe, the bishop received his copy of the book sometime during the middle nineties, it probably arrived while the leadership crisis at the church of Corinth was coming to a head; that crisis which occasioned Clement's famous epistle, a story told in *Four Witnesses*. There, peace had allowed an appetite for novelty to arise; and soon, a set of trendy usurpers from outside the original apostolic succession had taken charge. Rome itself was healthier in that regard, but even at Clement's own church, the comfortable frogs in the pot were, in Aesop's terms, beginning to lose track of the rising temperatures—as may be gathered from the pages of *The Shepherd* itself. The great patristics scholar Quasten writes:

> We meet here all classes of Christians—good as well as evil. We read of bishops, priests and deacons who have administered their office worthily before God, but also of priests who were given to judgment, proud, negligent and ambitious, and of deacons who had appropriated for themselves money intended for widows and orphans. . . . We are told of converts who are without stain of sin as well

---

[20] Ps 103:2–4.
[21] Cf. Mt 25:1–13.

as of all kinds of sinners; of wealthy persons who disdain poorer brethren and also of charitable and good Christians; of heretics as well as of doubters who struggle to find the way of righteousness; of good Christians with minor faults and of simulators and hypocrites. So the book of Hermas is a great self-examination on the part of the Church of Rome.[22]

If Clement began reading out of curiosity, kept going out of an increasing fondness for Hermas himself, and finally started taking the book seriously when its picture of conditions in his own diocese reflected the very worries that were likely keeping him up nights, then the passage that sealed the deal surely came in chapter 4. There, in an apparition highly reminiscent of the dragons and monsters that appear in St. John's Apocalypse—but in a section that may, in fact, *predate* the writing of that great book of Revelation (more on this later)—Hermas tells about the approach of a terrifying beast:

> I was going into the country by the Campanian Way. . . . [And] as I was walking by myself, I asked the Lord to complete the revelations and visions that he [had been showing] to me. . . . And I went on a little farther, brothers and sisters, and behold, I saw a cloud of dust rising up, as it were, to heaven, and I began to say to myself, "Maybe some cattle are coming and raising a cloud of dust?". . . [but] as the cloud of dust grew larger and larger, I began to suspect that it was something supernatural. Then the sun shone a little more brightly, and behold, I saw a huge beast, like some sea monster, and from its mouth flaming lo-

---

[22] Johannes Quasten, *Patrology* (Allen, Tex.: Christian Classics, 1986), 1:96–97.

custs were pouring out. And the beast was about one hundred feet long, and it had a head like a ceramic jar. And I began to cry and beg the Lord to rescue me from it. . . . And the beast was coming on with such a rush it could have destroyed a city.

Later, after an angel has turned the monster aside, Hermas is told:

"You deserved to escape it . . . because you cast your cares on God and opened your heart to the Lord, believing that you could not be saved by anything except the great and glorious Name. . . . You have escaped a great tribulation[23] because of your faith, and because you were not double-minded, even though you saw such a huge beast. Go, therefore, and declare to the Lord's elect his mighty works, and tell them that this beast is a foreshadowing of the great tribulation that is coming . . . [but that] if you prepare your heart in advance and turn to the Lord with all your heart, you will be able to escape it."[24]

Here, finally, must have been the passage that earned Hermas his hearing. Here, we can easily imagine, came the moment when Clement scrolled back to the beginning of the book and started over—reading, not as a critic now, but as a student.

Scared Straight

Whatever his other faults, Hermas the author is not slow coming to the point; time, after all, is short for a man who has seen a great new persecution coming on in a rush. Two sentences in to his celebrated book, he is already spilling

---

[23] Cf. Mt 24:21.
[24] Hermas, *Shepherd*, chap. 23, 4.2.

his guts to the reader about an embarrassing incident a less humble writer might well have tried to gloss over.

Some years, it seems, after being freed by Rhoda, Hermas —abandoned now by both wife and children—ran into his former owner again, both of them laypeople at the church of Rome. He began to love her—**"as a sister"**, he quickly assures us. **"Some time later I saw her bathing in the Tiber River, and I gave her my hand and helped her out of the river. When I saw her beauty I thought to myself and said, 'How happy I would be, if I had a wife of such beauty and character.' This was the only thing I thought, nothing more."** Nothing, in fact, came of the encounter; not on the earthly level, at any rate. Indeed, Rhoda died not long afterward; we do not know why. But soon after her death, as Hermas continues, **"I was going to Cumae and glorifying God's creatures for their greatness, splendor, and power, [and] I fell asleep as I walked. And a spirit took me and carried me away through a pathless region through which a man could not make his way, for the place was precipitous and eroded by the waters. When I had crossed the river, I came to level ground, and I knelt down and began to pray to the Lord and confess my sins."**

"While I was praying the heavens opened and I saw that woman whom I had desired greeting me from heaven, saying, 'Hello, Hermas.' And I stared at her and said, 'Lady, what are you doing here?' And she answered me, 'I have been taken up in order that I may accuse you of your sins before the Lord.'" Hermas is, of course, shocked and appalled. **"'God,'** Rhoda continues, **'who dwells in the heavens and created out of nothing the things that are, and increased and multiplied them for the sake of his holy**

church, is angry at you because you sinned against me.'
Answering her I said, 'I sinned against you? In what way?
Or when have I ever spoken an indecent word to you? Have
I not always regarded you as a goddess? Have I not always
respected you as a sister? Why do you falsely accuse me,
lady, of these evil and unclean things?' "

Hermas' inner thoughts seem to have betrayed him here;
who, after all, has mentioned anything indecent or unclean
up to this point?

"She laughed at me and said, 'The desire for evil rose up
in your heart. Or do you not think that it is an evil thing
for a righteous man if an evil desire rises up in his heart?' "
Rhoda's laughter is the laughter of the blessed. Like the wise
women in the fables of George MacDonald or the fantasies
of C.S. Lewis, she has passed far beyond personal resent-
ments now, and the joy of her present state overwhelms the
pettiness of all former concerns. The indictment she deliv-
ers is, however, a serious business, and it carries us back to
the words of the Savior Himself: "You have heard that it
was said, 'You shall not commit adultery.' But I say to you
that every one who looks at a woman lustfully has already
committed adultery with her in his heart" (Mt 5:27–28).
This rebuke from our Lord seems to have been occasioned,
as were so many others, by the degraded state of religion
He found in effect under the Pharisees, who, we learn from
their written expositions, insisted on interpreting the commandment against adultery very narrowly, so that no sexual
sin short of the finished act itself ought to be worrisome.
In fact, they went so far as blasphemously to cite Psalm
66:18 against it: "If I had cherished iniquity in my heart,
the Lord would not have listened." This Jesus contradicts

absolutely, insisting that even an adultery of the heart only, restrained by nothing except lack of a convenient opportunity for satisfaction, must not be confused with chastity. His Apostle James finishes the thought in chapter 1 of his great Epistle: **"Blessed is the man who endures trial, for when he has stood the test he will receive the crown of life which God has promised to those who love him. . . . Each person is tempted when he is lured and enticed by his own desire. Then desire when it has conceived gives birth to sin; and sin when it is full-grown brings forth death. Do not be deceived, my beloved brethren"** (Jas 1:12, 14–16).

Rhoda's startling words, like those of Christ Himself, are intended to pierce Hermas' outward shell of religiosity, to wake him from the Pharisaical spell of self-deception into which he has drifted. She concludes,

> **"It certainly is a sin, and a great one at that, . . . for the righteous aim at righteous things. So, then, as long as their aims are righteous, their reputation is secure in heaven and they find the Lord favorably inclined in all they do. But those who aim at evil things in their hearts bring death and captivity upon themselves, especially those who lay claim to this world and pride themselves on their wealth and do not hold fast to the good things that are to come. Their souls will regret it, for they have no hope; instead they have abandoned themselves and their life. But you, pray to God, and he will heal your sins, and those of your whole house, and of all the saints."**

Rhoda departs, leaving Hermas **"terribly shaken and upset"**. **"And I thought to myself, 'If even this sin is recorded against me, how can I be saved?'"** Later in the same dream,

Hermas is made to realize purpose behind the vision: **"You have been corrupted by the cares of this life. . . . But the great compassion of the Lord has had mercy on you"** and desires to **"strengthen you and establish you in his glory"**.

The second group of visions began a year later—and with them, the first prophecy of the coming conflagration. Walking again along the road to Cumae, Hermas reached the spot where he had seen Rhoda: **"And again a spirit took me and carried me away to the same place as the year before. So when I reached the place, I fell to my knees and began to pray to the Lord and to glorify his name because he had considered me worthy and had made known to me my former sins."** We see that Hermas, no longer arguing with God, has taken ownership of his earlier dream, realizing that it was sent to save, not to condemn. This response, indeed, is precisely what has made him worthy to become a vehicle for further revelations. In these new visions, Hermas becomes the student of a different woman, **"an elderly woman in a shining garment with a book in her hands"** sitting on **"a great white chair made of snow-white wool"**. Puzzled by the mystery of her identity, Hermas is enlightened by the appearance of an angelic-looking young man: **"She is the Church"**, the messenger informs him, **"and she seemed aged for she was created first of all things."**[25]

Now, the Lady herself begins to deliver her solemn warnings:

> **"Speak . . . to the officials of the church, in order that they may direct their ways in righteousness, in order**

---

[25] This line is taken from Marjorie Strachey's rendering in *The Fathers without Theology* (New York: Braziller, 1958), p. 20.

that they may receive the promises in full with much glory [and, indeed, it is within this context that she directs Hermas to write out a copy for Clement]. . . . Blessed are those of you who patiently endure the coming great tribulation and who will not deny their life. For the Lord has sworn by his Son that those who have denied their Lord have been rejected from their life, that is, those who now are about to deny him in the coming days. . . .[26]

"You, Hermas, have had great tribulations of your own because of the transgressions of your family, because you were not concerned about them. Instead, you neglected them and became entangled in your own evil transgressions. . . . But the great compassion of the Lord has had mercy on you and your family, and will strengthen you and establish you in his glory. Only do not be careless, but be courageous and strengthen your family. For just as the blacksmith by hammering at his work completes the task he wants to do, so also does the daily righteous word conquer all evil. Do not cease, therefore, instructing your children, for I know that if they repent with all their heart, they will be enrolled with the saints in the books of life.[27]

"After you have made known to them all these words, which the Master ordered me to reveal to you, then all the sins that they have previously committed will be forgiven them. Indeed, all the saints who have

---

[26] Cf. Mt 10:32–33: "So every one who acknowledges me before men, I also will acknowledge before my Father who is in heaven; but whoever denies me before men, I also will deny before my Father who is in heaven."

[27] Cf. Rev 3:5: "He who conquers shall be clothed like them in white garments, and I will not blot his name out of the book of life; I will confess his name before my Father and before his angels."

sinned up to this day will be forgiven, if they repent with all their heart and drive away double-mindedness from their heart."[28]

The time for casual Christianity, however, and for half-hearted discipleship has run out; once again, as in the days of the Baptizer, the Lord's winnowing fork is in His hand. **"For the Master has sworn by his own glory regarding his elect, that if sin still occurs, now that this day has been set as a limit, they will not find salvation . . . the days of repentance for all the saints are over."**

It was fifteen days after the last of these messages that Hermas was shown the vision of the sea monster. Afterward, he writes, **"a young lady met me dressed as if she were coming out of a bridal chamber, all in white and with white sandals, veiled down to her forehead, and her head covering was a turban, and her hair was white."** It takes Hermas a moment to realize that this is actually the same woman as before, the symbolic figure of the Church, her new vitality now signifying the message she brings, that any of her members **"who have fully repented . . . will be young and firmly established — those who repent with all their heart"**. **"So prepare yourselves in advance"**, she announces, **"Cast your cares upon the Lord, and he will set them straight. . . . Do not cease speaking to the ears of the saints. You have [seen] the great tribulation that is coming. But if you are willing, it will be nothing. Remember what has already been written."**

---

[28] Cf. Jas 4:8: "Draw near to God and he will draw near to you. Cleanse your hands, you sinners, and purify your hearts, you men of double mind."

"With these words she left," Hermas concludes, **"and I did not see where she went, for there was a noise, and I turned back in fear, thinking that the beast was coming."**

A Tower Built upon Water

At this point, it might be well to pause for a while and examine a few of the presuppositions embedded in what we have read so far; to address questions about how they came to be in place, why they are phrased exactly as they are, and what it means for today's Christians to find them here. Most specifically, we ought to investigate the strong note of danger we find in these early chapters of *The Shepherd* —warnings to "the Lord's elect", to "the saints", to people whose "reputation is secure in heaven . . . so long as their aims are righteous"—all indicating that it is possible for the backsliding Christian to sin so badly as to endanger his soul. Not all Evangelicals will have found this note unfamiliar (the very large Methodist/Holiness/Pentecostal/ Charismatic tradition follows John Wesley in this matter, an avid student of the Church Fathers), but it likely struck a jarring chord for any readers formed in the Calvinist school of "eternal security". As we indicated early on, the intent here is to try and shed additional light upon the controversy by reexamining the earliest records of the Church's beliefs on baptism, including the pages of Hermas' *Shepherd*.

Before imparting her glimpse of the great beast approaching, Hermas' Lady in white gave our visionary one other image to ponder: that of **"a great tower being built upon the waters"** to which the angels are continuously carrying stones to be considered for use in the project. Many of the stones were dragged from the deep and **"placed in the building just as they were, for they had been shaped and fit at the joints with the other stones. In fact, they fitted one another so closely that the joints were not visible, and the structure of the tower looked as if it were built of a single stone."** But other stones are brought in from the dry land; some of which, upon examination, are simply broken into pieces and discarded; others are tossed aside as too small or too round or otherwise-unsuitable for the job; and a few are dropped next to the water's edge, desiring to roll into the water but not quite able to do so.

"The tower that you see being built is I, the church," Hermas is told, and it is built upon water **"because your life was saved and will be saved through water."**[29] In what way? **"It was necessary"**, he learns, **"for [the stones] to come up through water in order to be made alive, for otherwise they could not enter the kingdom of God, unless they laid aside the deadness of their former life. . . . For before people bear the name of the Son of God . . . they are dead, but when they receive the seal, they lay aside their deadness and receive life. The seal, therefore, is the water; so they go down into the water dead and they come up alive."**[30] Those in the vision who fell near the water's edge but did not roll into it **"are the ones who**

---

[29] Cf. 1 Pet 3:20–21: ". . . [God waited patiently] in the days of Noah, during the building of the ark, in which a few, that is, eight persons, were saved through water. Baptism, which corresponds to this, now saves you, not as a removal of dirt from the body but as an appeal to God for a clear conscience, through the resurrection of Jesus Christ."

[30] Cf. Rom 6:4: "We were buried therefore with him by baptism into death, so that, as Christ was raised from the dead by the glory of the Father, so we too might walk in newness of life."

**heard the word and want to be baptized in the name of
the Lord, . . . [but] when they remember the purity of
truth, they change their minds and return again to their
evil desires."**[31] To summarize: baptism in water has become
the necessary vehicle for spiritual rebirth in Christ and for
admission into His Church, the kingdom of God.

Since Clement does not address baptism at all in his letter to the Corinthians, and since the *Didache* (or "Teaching
of the Twelve Apostles") gives only practical instructions
on how it is to be administered, this passage in Hermas'
Shepherd happens to stand as *our earliest statement on the topic
outside the pages of Scripture itself.* If the book, in other words,
contains doctrinal errors, it is certainly not because the passage of time, to cite the common metaphor, allowed barna-
cles to attach themselves to the ship. Hermas wrote while
men who had known the Apostles face-to-face were still
living to correct him, had he gone astray. And if the book
was, indeed, reviewed by one of the most prominent of
these, Clement of Rome, and passed along to the other
churches with his approval, then we may surely conclude
that nothing in its theology was seen as seriously amiss.
Likewise, the very wide welcome *The Shepherd* received in
the early Church can be taken as additional confirmation
of this.

---

[31] Cf. Mt 13:20–22: "As for what was sown on rocky ground, this is he
who hears the word and immediately receives it with joy; yet he has no root
in himself, but endures for a while, and when tribulation or persecution
arises on account of the word, immediately he falls away. As for what was
sown among thorns, this is he who hears the word, but the cares of the
world and the delight in riches choke the word, and it proves unfruitful."

Nor is there any discontinuity at all between Hermas' tower vision and the baptismal doctrine we find in the next wave of teachers, the great second- and third-century Fathers beginning with Justin Martyr, whose testimony on the topic we briefly reviewed in *Four Witnesses*: **"As many as are persuaded and believe that the things we teach and say are true, and undertake to live accordingly, . . . are born again in the same manner of rebirth by which we ourselves were born again,**[32] **for they then receive washing in water in the name of God the Father and Master of all, and of our Savior, Jesus Christ, and of the Holy Spirit."**[33] Please take care to notice that one of the most common misunderstandings of the traditional doctrine is already being addressed in this extremely early excerpt: yes, baptism is a true sacrament, a symbolic ritual that actually accomplishes the thing it symbolizes; it is given, nevertheless, *only to those who have made a prior profession of faith.* So baptism, it is true, is necessary for salvation, but faith is necessary for baptism.[34]

---

[32] Cf. Jn 3:5, 7 (KJV): "'Verily, verily, I say unto thee, Except a man be born of water and of the Spirit, he cannot enter into the kingdom of God. . . . Marvel not that I said unto thee, Ye must be born again."

[33] Justin Martyr, *First Apology*, chap. 61, Ancient Christian Writers (hereafter abbreviated ACW), vol. 56 (Mahwah, N.J.: Paulist Press, 1948), p. 66.

[34] Yet how does faith come in as part of an *infant* baptism—a practice that can be shown to have been employed by the early Church from the earliest days of her existence? "Is the New law to be less perfect than the Old," asks Catholic apologist Fr. Leslie Rumble, "containing no purifying rite for infants?" In the case of an unconscious child, incapable of personal faith until he reaches the age of reason, the Church has always seen a parallel (introduced by St. Paul in Colossians 1) to the ancient rite of circumcision. Just as an Israelite was made heir to God's promises by "riding the coattails", so to speak, of his family's faith, so does the child of

Similar affirmations might be multiplied indefinitely: Irenaeus, Tertullian, Hippolytus, Clement of Alexandria, Origen, Cyril of Jerusalem, Cyprian of Carthage—all make strong statements in support of the sacramental nature of water baptism, its necessity for salvation under ordinary circumstances, and its traditional identification with regeneration and new birth. Most significant of all, however, is the near-absolute absence of any contrary testimony. Look as we may for another opinion—for some early Christian writer who might wish to deny the necessity of baptism or its sacramental efficacy or to affirm, instead, a new birth by faith alone without any physical instrumentalities—we find instead only unquestioned agreement all around. This oneness of mind on baptism, in fact, is one of the most striking discoveries to be made in the entire record of early Christianity; and it cannot, historically speaking, be gainsaid at all without resort to some conspiracy theory.

Faith in the divine power of baptism was so strong and so universal, in fact, that it seems actually to have become a practical problem by Hermas' day. Already, in his vision of the Tower, we find baptism referred to as **"the seal of eternal life"**, and other, later Fathers expand on that uplifting theme in ways that really might begin to suggest the later conception of "once saved, always saved": **"Bearing your**

---

a Christian family become—via "the circumcision of Christ" (Col 2:11) —the beneficiary of graces not yet strictly his own. It is also the teaching of the Church, however, that the new life of the spirit gained in baptism will prove stillborn unless the recipient of that sacrament embraces *actual, personal faith* for himself when that does become possible. One can inherit the initial "jump start" from one's parents, in other words, but no one ever does go to heaven solely on someone else's faith.

sins," writes Cyril, "you go down into the water; but the calling down of grace seals your soul and does not permit that you afterwards be swallowed up by the fearsome dragon. You go down dead in your sins, and you come up made alive in righteousness."[35] This note, while valid and true, was and is subject to overemphasis; especially at times when peace has produced the state of affairs we have already seen at Clement's Rome . . . and at Clement's Corinth as well. St. Paul himself, recall, addressed exactly the same situation at that same church of Corinth some thirty-five years earlier: widespread, blasé reliance upon not just the seal of baptism but on the restorative powers of the Eucharistic bread and cup as well, from a community grown lax, quarrelsome, and broadly tolerant of sexual immorality:

> I want you to know, brethren, that our fathers were all . . . baptized into Moses in the cloud and in the sea, and all ate the same supernatural food and all drank the same supernatural drink. For they drank from the supernatural Rock which followed them, and the Rock was Christ. Nevertheless with most of them God was not pleased; for they were overthrown in the wilderness. . . . [A]s it is written, "The people sat down to eat and drink and rose up to dance." We must not indulge in immorality as some of them did, and twenty-three thousand fell in a single day. We must not put the Lord to the test, as some of them did and were destroyed by serpents; nor grumble, as some of them did and were destroyed by the Destroyer. Now these things happened to them as a warning, but they were written down for our instruction, upon whom the end of the

---

[35] *FEF* 1:349, no. 812.

ages has come. Therefore let any one who thinks that
he stands take heed lest he fall. (1 Cor 10:1–5, 7b–12)

This note, too, is practically universal in the early Church.
The *Didache*, written as scholars believe while most of the
Apostles were still active, advises us to *"Watch* **over your
life;** *your lamps* **must not go out, nor** *your loins* **be un-
girded; on the contrary,** *be ready. You do not know the hour
in which our Lord is coming.* **Assemble in great numbers, intent upon what concerns your souls. Surely, of no use will
your lifelong faith be to you if you are not perfected at the
end of time."**[36] And the *Epistle of Barnabas*, composed, most
probably, while Hermas was still a layman at Rome, warns
**"Do not shut yourselves up and court solitude as though
your justification were already assured. On the contrary,
attend the common meetings and join in discussing what
contributes to the common good. For the Scripture says,**
*Ruin awaits those who are wise in their own estimation and
prudent in their own conceit. . . .*[37] **Let us never rest, on the
ground that we have been called, or fall asleep in our sins;
may the wicked Ruler never gain power over us and force
us away from the kingdom of the Lord."**[38]

The seal or mark of baptism itself is not lost; indeed, it
is the very thing that gives the sinning Christian access to
the power of confession and restoration. In this sense, the
Calvinist is not wrong to insist "once a Christian, always a
Christian". **"[The] invisible seal of the Spirit is impressed
on our bodies",** writes St. Ephraim the Syrian, **"with the**

---

[36] *The Didache*, ACW, no. 6 (1978), p. 24.
[37] Is 5:21.
[38] *The Epistle of Barnabas*, ACW, no. 6, pp. 41–42.

oil with which we are anointed in Baptism, whereby we
bear His seal."[39] "No sin can erase this mark", according
to the *Catechism of the Catholic Church*, "even if sin prevents
Baptism from bearing the fruits of salvation" (*CCC* 1272).
Summarizing the testimony of later Fathers such as Athanasius and Augustine, Catholic scholar Fr. John Hardon explains it this way: "[Baptism] imparts to those who receive
it a likeness to Christ in his priesthood, grafts them onto
Christ, the Vine, so that they participate in a unique way
in the graces of his humanity. It imprints on their souls an
indelible seal that nothing, not even the loss of virtue or
faith itself, can eradicate. . . . A baptized person always remains a Christian because the baptismal character confers
a permanent relationship with Christ. . . . The seal of baptism continues in this life and endures into eternity."[40]

This explains how Hermas himself can write thus, recording additional elucidations of the tower vision:

> Those who do not know God [i.e., the unbaptized] and
> do evil receive some punishment for their evil, but
> those who have come to know God ought no longer
> to do evil, but to do good. So if those who ought to
> do good do evil, do they not appear to do greater evil
> than those who do not know God? This is why those
> who have not known God and do evil are condemned
> to death, whereas those who have known God and
> have seen his mighty works and yet do evil will be

---

[39] *FEF* 1:313, no. 712. The Church inherited the use of consecrated oils
during certain rites from the Old Testament priesthood.

[40] Fr. John Hardon, *The Question & Answer Catholic Catechism* (New York:
Image Books, 1981), pp. 233–34.

doubly punished and will die forever.[41] In this way, therefore, the church of God will be purified.[42]

When John the Baptist came offering one last chance to **"flee from the wrath to come"**, those who second-guessed the need for such a harsh message were warned to **"Bear fruit that befits repentance, and do not presume to say to yourselves, 'We have Abraham as our father'; for I tell you, God is able from these stones to raise up children to Abraham"** (Mt 3:7–9). The Roman Christians who first read *The Shepherd* were treading, it seems, a very similar path; trusting in the rite of baptism alone (God-established though it was) in just the same way the lazy Israelites had come to rely on circumcision (equally God-established) and mere physical descent from their patriarch, Abraham. *The Shepherd*, then, was likely quite a shock—which would certainly explain how it came to be so famous, so fast, even without apostolic origins. Yet if the dangers to the backsliding Christian are clear in Hermas' vision, so is the infallible efficacy of confession and forgiveness—and their easy accessibility.

"Go and speak to all the people", Hermas is told, **"in order that they may repent and live to God, for the Lord in his compassion [wishes] to give repentance to all."** Those who do confess their iniquities and turn from wrongdoing,

---

[41] Cf. Lk 12:47–48: "And that servant who knew his master's will, and did not make ready or act according to his will, shall receive a severe beating. But he who did not know, and did what deserved a beating, shall receive a light beating. Every one to whom much is given, of him will much be required; and of him to whom men commit much they will demand the more."

[42] Hermas, *Shepherd*, 9.18, *Apostolic Fathers*, p. 277.

"will receive healing from the Lord for their previous sins". "Many will hear," the White Lady predicts, "but after hearing, some of them will rejoice, but others will weep. Yet even these, if they hear and repent, will also rejoice."[43] Even the stones that were tossed aside, she says, "were not thrown far from the tower, because they will be useful for building if they repent. . . . They will be strong in faith if they repent now while the tower is still being built." "If, however, any are about to repent, let them do so quickly, before the tower is completed."[44] The coming of the sea monster has turned a hobby, an aspiration, a "New Year's Resolution". . . into a matter of life and death.

Enter the Shepherd

When the tribulation came as predicted, it was great indeed, for it lasted *one hundred and sixty-four years*, a period during which brutal, state-sponsored persecution of Christians broke out regularly within the empire, but private or local mob-based violence and bigotry appear to have been practically continuous. No, Hermas' tribulation did not turn out to be the *final* tribulation, any more than the antichrist Domitian with whom the period began turned out to be *the* final antichrist; but Christians of that era did not, of course, know this in advance, lacking our 20/20 hindsight. To us, the fact that the early Church was persecuted is a truism; to those who first read *The Shepherd*, it was a shocking prophecy coming true before their eyes.

---

[43] Ibid., 8.11, p. 263; 3.3, p. 213.
[44] Ibid., 9.26, p. 281; 3.5, p. 215.

It was Domitian who exiled St. John to the island of Patmos around the year 95, where that beloved disciple experienced the visions that are recorded in the book of Revelation (meaning, incidentally, that it is entirely possible Hermas wrote first, though not by much, of course). John gives witness therein to the initial outbreak, sharing Christ's praise to the church at Pergamum for **"[holding] fast my name and you did not deny my faith even in the days of Antipas my witness, my faithful one, who was killed among you, where Satan dwells"** (Rev 2:13). Clement survived to see the beginning as well; apologizing, at the start of his letter to the Corinthians, for his tardiness in addressing their disorders, owing **"to the sudden and successive calamitous events which have happened to ourselves"** ("ourselves" being a group that included Hermas, his parishioner). Our much-loved Ignatius of Antioch, second witness in our original roll call, was haled to the bar of Trajan's justice less than a decade later and fed to the lions at the bloody Coliseum. Christians in the Holy Land were ordered to swear allegiance to Simon Bar Kochba in 135 and to take an oath that he, not Jesus of Nazareth, was the true Hebrew Messiah; they fled to the hills, instead, to escape the final destruction of Jerusalem and endured great hardship while homeless there.[45] Justin the Martyr was beheaded around 155, early in the persecution of Marcus Aurelius; the same emperor was on the throne in 177 when Blandina and her

---

[45] More insight into these events and their meaning for the early Church may be gleaned from this author's *Scripture Wars: Justin Martyr's Battle to Save the Old Testament for Christians* (Manchester, N.H.: Sophia Institute Press, 2019).

companions, part of Irenaeus' heroic flock, bore witness to the holy name of Jesus at Lyons. Perpetua and Felicity suffered under Septimius Severus early in the third century; Clement's successor, Pontian, was exiled in 235; the persecution of Decius in 250 was so severe that it produced hundreds of Christian apostates, just as Hermas had feared; and Sts. Cyprian, Sixtus II, and Lawrence were among the famous victims of Valerian in 253. It was Valerian's son, Galerius, who finally called the whole thing off in exhaustion, issuing the very first edict of toleration for Christianity in 259, allowing churches to operate openly. Yes, there were a few lulls along the way—but for the Church undergoing it, all this was experienced as one cataclysmic, multigenerational event.

What became of Hermas himself once all his dreams started coming true? The answer to that question depends largely on how one goes about dating his book. The reference to Clement, Hermas' bishop in Rome, who will, according to the White Lady, send important information to the churches abroad **"because that is his job"**, would seem to be clear enough. Yet several other ancient sources maintain that *The Shepherd* was published during the bishopric of Pius I, who sat on the chair of Peter from about 140 to 155—at least forty years after Clement's death. This seeming contradiction has sometimes led scholars to jump to the conclusion that Hermas' invocation of Clement's name is a fictional device. "There is", however, according to Quasten, "no valid reason why it should be so labelled. The two dates are accounted for by the way in which the book was compiled. The older portions would most likely go back to Clement's day while the present redaction would be of Pius'

time."[46] If Hermas was thirty in the year 95, he would have
been about seventy-five in 140; a life-span quite within the
realm of possibility. Likewise, the book itself is clearly divided into two parts, with a definite change of tone in the
second half. The theology there seems more developed, and
several passages do, now, appear to reflect a familiarity with
St. John's later writings. The most natural way to approach
this is to infer that Hermas survived the early waves of persecution . . . and lived to amplify and amend his advice in
response to more recent developments.

Those more recent troubles centered once again around
the sacrament of baptism: not, oddly enough, over whether
baptism saves, this time, but whether anything else can.
During the tribulation, the problem was no longer that
of a slumbering laity needing to be alerted to the lateness
of the hour but that of a battle-hardened minority of survivors and confessors now inclined toward rigorism and the
taking of "a hard line" in matters of forgiveness. Having
seen their loved ones killed by the score rather than sacrifice to the gods, they now had to watch as Christians who
had sacrificed rather than face torture and death professed
themselves "sorry" for what they had done and started asking to be readmitted to fellowship. By the time of Pius,
these grumbling diehards seem to have begun taking Hermas' original message of "one last chance before the tribulation" and interpreting it as "one chance, period". Some
even went beyond this to deny that forgiveness for serious
sin is even possible after baptism. This denial was not, mind
you, formulated in the later, familiar Calvinist terms, i.e.,

---

[46] Quasten, *Patrology*, 1:92.

that one who apostatizes or commits very serious sin does not actually lose his salvation but only reveals that he was never truly saved to begin with. No, the early Church's universal faith in the efficacy of baptism was far too strong to allow for that kind of explanation. The fact that the famous second- and third-century rigorists such as Montanus and Novatian never used it is a testimony to that reality. These insisted quite explicitly that *baptism alone* has the power to save and that post-baptismal sin in a very grave matter produces an actual forfeiture of divine grace from which there is no return.

So, in the second half of his book, the now-elderly Hermas reveals another set of visions; brought by a new messenger. **"After I had prayed in my house and sat down on my bed, there came a man glorious in appearance, dressed like a shepherd, with a white skin wrapped around him and with a bag on his shoulders and a staff in his hand."** Here at last is the character after which the whole book has come to be named, a being who later identifies himself as **"the angel of repentance"**. **"I was sent"**, the Shepherd explains, **"that I might show you again everything that you saw previously, the most important points, those useful to you."**[47]

Among many other lessons, the Shepherd addresses the problem of **"hypocrites [who have] brought in strange doctrines, and perverted God's servants, especially the ones who had sinned, by not allowing them to repent, but dissuading them instead with their moronic doctrines."**[48]

---

[47] Hermas, *Shepherd*, Vision 5 [25].5.
[48] Ibid., 8.6, p. 261.

True Christians, in other words, who had sinned by apostasy and in other life-threatening ways, were turning away from the Church in despair, having been told by heretics that their condition was now hopeless. To these, the Shepherd says, **"I am in charge of repentance, and I give understanding to all who repent. . . . For since the Lord knows every heart and knows everything in advance, he knew the weakness of human beings and the cunning of the devil, and that he would do something evil to God's servants and treat them wickedly. The Lord, however, who is exceedingly merciful, had mercy on his creation and established this opportunity for repentance, and authority over this repentance was given to me."** Even with such a liberal proclamation of clemency, however, penitents would obviously, given the situation at the time, have had difficulty coming back into the fold simply on their own recognizance; deciding for themselves, that is, when their repentance had been genuine enough to merit restoration. The very fact that *The Shepherd* depicts the lapsed coming to the officers of the Church asking to be readmitted shows that they realized the clergy would have to be involved somehow —as all the early records show that they were.

Clement's letter to Corinth shows a system of penance in place during the earliest stage of the tribulation, exhorting the rebels there to **"Be subject in obedience to the priests [*presbyteris*] and receive discipline [*correctionem*] unto penance, bending the knees of your hearts."** A decade or so later, Ignatius of Antioch warns the wavering Philadelphians to return **"with one consent to the unity of Christ"**, reminding them that **"the bishop presides over penance"**. And Irenaeus, dealing with a group of women who had fallen away into a gnostic cult but later had second thoughts, tells us that some were willing **"to make a public confession, but others are ashamed to do this, and in silence, as if withdrawing from themselves the hope of the life of God, they either apostatize entirely or hesitate between the two courses."** In all of these quotes—from three of our four earliest witnesses, mind you—we can see that "the performance of penance was required", as the Catholic scholar E. Hanna writes, "and the nature of that penance was determined, not by the penitent himself, but by ecclesiastical authority." Cyprian of Carthage, addressing those who fell away during the Decian persecution, strongly rebukes them, but also spells out the Church's prescribed remedy: **"Let each confess his sin while he is still in this world, while his confession can be received, while satisfaction and the forgiveness granted by the priests is acceptable to God."**[49]

Where did the Church's officers obtain this miraculous capacity to remit someone else's sins? From Christ Himself, of course, who passed it down to the Apostles from His Father: **"[H]e breathed on them, and said to them, 'Receive the Holy Spirit. If you forgive the sins of any, they are forgiven; if you retain the sins of any, they are retained"** (Jn 20:22–24). And like their authority to teach on His behalf and to baptize all nations, this was a power intended to be transmitted to their own successors as a permanent institution in the Church. That this authority encompassed

---

[49] All citations in this paragraph are quoted in the article "Penance" in *CE*: www.newadvent.org/cathen/11618c.htm, except the quotation from Irenaeus, which is taken from his *Against Heresies* 1:22.

all types of sin, no matter how serious, can be proved from a passage in Eusebius' *Church History* summarizing the policy of Bishop Dionysius of Corinth, who wrote about the same as Irenaeus: **"And writing to the church that is in Amastris, together with those in Pontus, he . . . commands them to receive those who come back again after any fall, whether it be delinquency or heresy."**[50]

Yet notice, too, that Christ's commission to forgive sins includes the authority to *retain* them as well—to determine, that is, that any given penitent may not be ready to receive absolution just yet. This usually meant that there was some doubt about the sincerity or the completeness of his confession, over whether the subject was actually sorry for what he had done or just sorry to be experiencing the consequences. Origen (about whom much more will be said later) writes of the **"severe and arduous pardon of sins by penance, when the sinner washes his couch with tears, and when he blushes not to disclose his sin to the priest of the Lord and seeks the remedy [after the manner of (David) who said, 'To the Lord I will accuse myself of iniquity' (cf. Ps 32:5)]."**[51] These penances usually took the form of a period of fasting, of extra prayer and works of service, and other methods of proving out the sincerity of a penitent's aims—not just in the eyes of the clergy, but before the rest of the flock as well. Why should these mortifications be any of the congregation's business? Not just for nosiness, much less done for the satisfaction of the vin-

---

[50] Eusebius, *Church History*, 4:23, online at www.newadvent.org/fathers/250104.htm.

[51] Origen, Homily "In Levit.", ii, 4 (*PG* 12:418), quoted in "Sacrament of Penance", *CE*: www.newadvent.org/cathen/11618c.htm.

dictive, this public quality actually served a terribly practical purpose. There was an all-too-pressing need for each individual church to assure herself that persons who had already turned traitor in the past would not sell out their brethren again to avoid trouble in the future. Even in matters less grim, however, the probationary quality of these periods of penance served a crucial role in hindering this holy sacrament from being perverted into license to sin. Repeat offenders and other insincere petitioners would, like Irenaeus' gnostic women, often dally with the idea of returning to communion with the Church but end up balking at the required exertions.

The Shepherd, at any rate, "the angel of repentance" himself, made the necessity of acting out one's contrition in many cases very clear to Hermas at an early date. Even those who have **"repented with all their heart"** must sometimes, in his words, **"torment their own soul and be extremely humble in everything they do and be afflicted with a variety of afflictions"**. If they do, **"then assuredly the one who created all things . . . will be moved with compassion and will give some healing"**—and not just restoration, but increased power to endure temptation going forward.[52]

Shepherd of the Adulterers

Ironically, the most famous notice of *The Shepherd* from antiquity is a nasty label put upon it by Tertullian, perhaps the most renowned of all early Christian writers. Readers of *Four Witnesses* may recall that Tertullian, always a harsh

---

[52] Hermas, *Shepherd*, pp. 255–56.

and excessive personality even while still a Catholic, broke
with the apostolic Church around 207 and joined the Montanists. Montanus himself, founder of the cult, was already
dead by that time; but his devotees—including, now, Tertullian—continued to revere him as an incarnation of the
Holy Spirit and to venerate his recorded sayings on the same
par with actual Scripture. Because mainstream Christianity
had failed to acknowledge this alleged inspiration, the followers of Montanus began to look for ways to criticize it
as harshly as possible—which led them into a malicious,
holier-than-thou brand of rigorism that, alas, suited Tertullian's critical nature to a tee. The wit and virulence he had
once employed against persecutors and pagan philosophy
he now turned against the orthodox faith; and no display
of severity or strictness was too extreme. Readmission of
fallen-away sinners, needless to say, via sacramental confession and penance, became the ultimate proof of his former
communion's hopeless interior rot. This was the point at
which Hermas' *Shepherd* (a book which, by the way, Tertullian had previously cited as "Scripture") now became **the
Shepherd of the adulterers**.[53]

This is also how Tertullian became, paradoxically, one
of the best, most reliable witnesses to what the apostolic
Church actually taught on this important subject—best because most unwilling. The testimonies of hostile witnesses,
as apologist Gary Michuta writes, "are the best kind of evidence because they cannot be said to reflect bias in favor

---

[53] Tertullian, *On the Resurrection*, quoted in the *Oxford Dictionary of the
Christian Church*, ed. F. L. Cross (Oxford: Oxford University Press, 2005),
p. 764.

of the faith or the Church—quite the opposite, in fact."[54]
Tertullian expressed his basic doctrine on baptism in a treatise written prior to his defection to Montanism, nor did it
change after the revolt: **"Baptism is itself a corporal act by
which we are plunged in water, while its effect is spiritual,
in that we are freed from sins."**[55] But his shameless defense
afterward of the Montanist denials proves out what the apostolic Church believed on reconciliation as well as anything
could. When Callistus, bishop of Rome from 218 to 222,
published an edict on the topic (**"I forgive the sins of adultery and fornication to those who have done penance"**),
Tertullian admits that he once held the same belief, but **"I
blush not at an error which I have cast off because I am delighted at being rid of it . . . one is not ashamed of his own
improvement."** The "error" with which he now charges
Callistus (along with the entire non-Montanist Church, a
hundred times the size of his own) is nothing else but the
orthodox belief of his day—the Church's power, that is, to
forgive or to retain all sins. When confronted with a passage in his earlier discourse titled *Antidote to the Scorpion*,
in which Tertullian affirmed a bishop's power to forgive all
sins because **"the Lord left to Peter, and through him to
the Church the keys of heaven"**, he simply denies, once
again, what he had formerly professed—in company with
the whole of apostolic Christianity. Most paradoxically of
all, Tertullian eventually found it necessary to assert that the
Montanist schism, being the "true remnant", *did* actually
possess this power of the keys, having received it by way

[54] Gary Michuta, *Hostile Witnesses* (El Cajon, Calif.: Catholic Answers
Press, 2016), p. 12.
[55] *FEF* 1:127, no. 304.

of "the Paraclete" (Montanus); whom he quotes as having said: " 'The Church can forgive sin, but I will not do that (forgive) lest they (who are forgiven) fall into other sins.' "[56] A more thorough admission of the final futility of Tertullian's stance can hardly be conceived.

Mention of Montanus, however, does raise an interesting question—and here is where The Shepherd's role in helping to bring about the close of the New Testament canon comes in. Both Montanus and Hermas were private seers; both claimed to be relaying messages from God. Both sets of messages seem to have been held as scriptural by many on that basis alone—they liked or approved of the content, in other words. On what basis did the apostolic Church welcome (or at least linger over) the visions of Hermas, while quickly tarring those of Montanus as profane or unorthodox?

We can gain some light on this question by examining the parallel case of the book of Revelation, which was beginning to be examined about the same time. Most of the Western Fathers (including Melito, Irenaeus, and Hippolytus) readily accepted it as the inspired work of St. John the Apostle; in the East, however, there was a good deal more doubt during the early centuries and even resistance (from writers like Dionysius and Cyril). Many thought that it was simply too strange to be what it purported to be, too unlike anything else in the collection of books already agreed upon up to that point. Even hundreds of years later,

---

[56] All of Tertullian's quotes in this paragraph are taken from the article "The Sacrament of Penance", at catholic.org/encyclopedia/view.php?id= 9880.

Protestant founder Martin Luther—always quick to "trust his gut" above any existing traditions or authorities—was still experiencing similar doubts: "About this book of the Revelation of John, I leave everyone free to hold his own opinion. . . . [I, myself,] consider it to be neither apostolic nor prophetic. First and foremost, the [real] apostles do not deal with visions, but prophesy in clear and plain words, as do Peter and Paul, and Christ in the gospel. . . . I can in no way detect that the Holy Spirit produced it. . . . I stick to the books which present Christ to me clearly and purely."[57] Happily, cooler heads prevailed, and Dr. Luther's successors declined to follow him into these speculations; Lutheran Bibles still include the book of Revelation (along with Esther, James, and Hebrews—other books that their founder doubted). In fact, we may turn to Luther's own immediate successor, Andreas Carlstadt, for a shortcut to the ultimate answer; the method by means of which the early Church did, finally, complete the project: "One must appeal either to known apostolic authorship or to universal historical acceptance as to the test of a book's canonicity, not to internal doctrinal considerations."[58] Trying, in other words, to decide on our own which books "sound" like the Word of God actually amounts to nothing more than the old proverbial "fox guarding the henhouse".

Christians are supposed to get their ideas of truth *from* the Bible—not judge the truth *of* what may, in fact, be a biblical

---

[57] This short preface appeared in the September Testament of 1522 and in other editions up to 1527. It was supplanted from 1530 on by a much longer preface that offers an interpretation of the symbolism of the book. www.bible-researcher.com/antilegomena.html.

[58] Carlstadt, *De Canonicis Scripturis libellus* (Wittenberg, 1520), p. 50.

book by their own merely human notions. Jesus, we must
never forget, told the Apostles: **"Whoever listens to you listens to me; whoever rejects you rejects me; but whoever
rejects me rejects him who sent me."**[59] Christ, in other
words, taught with God's own authority, and He commissioned His ambassadors to do the same. Thus, "apostolic
authorship" becomes the key criterion. This is the sense
in which Christians believe the New Testament books to
be "God's Holy Word"—not because they, themselves, fell
down from heaven (they did not), but because of *who wrote
or authorized them*. This, after all, is why the books were circulated in the churches to begin with: they were copied and
read aloud during worship because they were considered sacred—a living link to the Apostles and, through them, to
Jesus Christ.

A case like that of Hermas, however, challenged the
Church to parse out her thoughts a bit further. Just how
apostolic did a book have to be to be considered an apostolic book? Peter, James, John, and others of the original
Twelve were obviously foundational—as was Paul, whose
epistles had been in use in the churches from the beginning,
as everyone agreed. Mark and Luke (not part of the Twelve)
made the cut because their Gospels were likewise unquestioned and were generally considered to have been overseen
by Peter and Paul, respectively. But what of the *Epistle to the
Hebrews*, which seemed always to have been linked to the
name Paul somehow but was not written in his easily recognizable style (Tertullian believed Barnabas was the author—
one of several "apostles with a small 'a'" whom we meet in

---

[59] Lk 10:16, NIV.

the book of Acts). Beyond this, the candidates trailed away in concentric circles, fading at last into shades of gray. Was Ignatius Theophorus an "apostolic man"—ordained as he was by Peter to be bishop at Antioch? Might Clement of Rome not be considered an "apostle" after the manner of Luke or Barnabas—since he seems to have been as much a "fellow worker" of Paul's as they? And if so, perhaps Hermas, also, whose book Clement appears to have sanctioned, had stood close enough to capture "a little of the *gloria*"?

Hermas, after all, had several advantages Montanus lacked. Not only did his connection to Clement count for a great deal, but his book *The Shepherd* had been genuinely embraced by the Church since the time of Clement—by *the apostolic churches*, mind you, the ones that so quickly rejected Montanus "the Paraclete". Even the book of Revelation itself had not yet gained such a widespread welcome. Probably this happened because the prophecies contained in *The Shepherd* appeared to have been ratified by events so dramatically. For those who had taken its message to heart, the book may even have been life-saving—*soul-saving*, in fact—with sheer gratitude on their parts going a long way toward explaining its curious popularity during the second century. Still, the Church hesitated. Would the biblical canon not *have* to close at some point in time, of necessity? Would apostolicity not eventually lose *all* of its ginger, at third hand or perhaps six degrees of separation? And yet, if *The Shepherd* had worked such a glorious miracle of deliverance as was generally conceded, do we dare, like the Pharisees, to attribute that miracle to Beelzebul—to a voice crying " **'Thus says the Lord God,' when the Lord has not spoken**" (Ezek 22:28)? To put the matter shortly: If *The Shepherd* truly contains the

Word of God, then must it not be proclaimed as Scripture, *ipso facto*? But if, contrariwise, it is not Scripture, does that not make Hermas a false prophet?

We get just a fleeting glimpse, it is believed, of one early Father desperate to escape this merciless conundrum —a very instructive mistake. Origen of Alexandria, writing about 230, made an otherwise inexplicable attempt to identify the author of *The Shepherd* with the biblical Hermas mentioned in Romans 16:14; a personage about whom nothing, really, is known, beyond the fact that he was a Roman acquaintance of St. Paul with a very common Greek name. Origen's effort is inexplicable, chronologically speaking, because the Letter to the Romans was written *not later than* A.D. *58*; a date that would render our own Hermas' well-attested survival into the era of Pius I wholly impossible. Origen was grasping at straws, then; frantic to save a book he is known to have loved, which the great Irenaeus had called Scripture, trying pretty much anything to vindicate *The Shepherd*'s widespread acceptance by finding good old Joe Schmoe some apostolic credentials in at least *some* sense of the term, somewhere, somehow.

What was actually needed to resolve this dilemma— without resorting to such tomfoolery—was some method for acknowledging the existence of "a message from God" without implying that all postapostolic prophecies must now be copied out onto the blank pages at the back of our Bibles. And as pressure grew to complete the final, official list of New Testament books—due to the promulgation of false, "alternative" canons created by heretical groups like the Gnostics and Marcionites—the apostolic Church was at last driven to think the issue out to a finish.

"Do not quench the Spirit, do not despise prophesying." Though the free-lance prophecies of early times are often described as having gradually died out, even Eusebius, writing some two hundred years after Hermas, bears witness that they still played a role even in his day. No, what actually happened is that the Fathers gradually learned to make a clear distinction between *officially* revealed truth intended for the entire Church—the *depositum fidei*, or "deposit of faith", left behind by her apostolic founders[60]— and private revelations made directly by God to individuals, binding only on those to whom they are given. God retains His freedom to speak whenever and to whomever He chooses; but these communications are never intended to complete or amend the deposit, which was actually complete at the end of the apostolic age. The canon of Scripture closed when the last living Apostle died, losing his ability to write or to authorize any more. In churches of the Catholic tradition, no one's conscience is bound to accept anything that was not part of the original *depositum fidei* — not the opinion of any pope, the writings of any saint, or the visions (however well attested) at Lourdes or Fatima. And all our individual intuitions, no matter how compelling, must always be checked against the written Word of God. But from Martin of Tours to Antony of the Desert, from Francis of Assisi to Paisios of Mount Athos, right up to the

---

[60] "St. Paul uses the Greek word 'paratheke' [*depositum*, in Latin] . . . meaning something precious entrusted to a depositary for safekeeping [when he says, in 1 Timothy 6:20] 'O Timothy, guard [what has been entrusted to you'; and again in 2 Timothy 1:14 'Guard this rich trust with the help of the holy Spirit that dwells within us.']": Msgr. Eugene Kevane, ewtn.com/catholicism/library/deposit-of-faith-and-the-priesthood-11919.

personal consolations many ordinary Christians have experienced from a "still, small voice" or in a charismatic manifestation—private visions and messages have continued to come and will continue to come, resonating in the hearts of millions. Just as they did in the personal revelations to "Joe Schmoe" more than nineteen centuries ago.

He was not an Apostle—or even a clergyman at all. Neither his book nor the content of his dreams were binding on anyone, not then and not now. But for those who had ears to hear, Hermas was certainly a blessing. He serves as a witness to what doctrines would and would not fly in the apostolic churches of A.D. 140.

And in his own way, grouchy old Tertullian was correct as well. Catholic Christians really do follow "the Shepherd of the Adulterers"—thanks be to God! Christ Jesus, the Good Shepherd, **"came into the world to save sinners"** (1 Tim 1:15), even those whose adulteries may have happened only in the heart. It was He who taught us to pray daily that our Father might **"forgive us our trespasses, as we forgive those who trespass against us"** (Mt 6:12). And it was He who inspired his Apostle John to write: **"If we say we have no sin, we deceive ourselves, and the truth is not in us. If we confess our sins, he is faithful and just, and will forgive our sins and cleanse us from all unrighteousness"** (1 Jn 1:8–9).

Clement of Alexandria

When his stagecoach finally came rumbling into Alexandria (they called them *raeda* in those days, wooden horse-drawn wagons with noisy iron-shod wheels), it was the culmination of a journey of years, a tour of practically the whole of ancient Christendom. Though the details are few, his surviving books refer to extensive travels in southern Europe, in Asia (as the Romans used to call what is now Turkey), in Syria, and the Holy Land. And during the course of this voyage—which took place, by the way, during the decade of the 180s—he visited congregation after congregation, and **"was privileged"**, he tells us, **"to hear [the discourses] of blessed and truly remarkable men"**.[1]

He went looking for the Church, did Titus Flavius Clemens—not just her body or her members, but her *mind*, the mind of Christ. Jesus Himself, after all, called it the great and first commandment: **"You shall love the Lord your God with all your heart, and with all your soul, and with all your mind"** (Mt 22:37). This, for a man like Clement (second by that name in our narrative and not to be confused with Hermas' bishop, Clement of Rome), was going to be quite a job, for his mind was prodigious. St. Jerome, in fact, called Clement the most learned of all the ancients. But his path began at *Athens*, not just literally, but figuratively

---

[1] Clement of Alexandria, *The Stromata* 1,1,11 www.newadvent.org/father s/02101.htm.

as well; which means that Clement was born into paganism, at the very heart of it, and steeped in the Attic poets
and philosophers. His conversion to Christianity, therefore
(about which we have no details—not even a date), was the
starting gun for a major reclamation project: to **"take every
thought captive to obey Christ"** as St. Paul wrote (2 Cor
10:5); and to **"Put off the old man that belongs to your
former manner of life . . . and be renewed in the spirit of
your minds"** (Eph 4:22–23). Clement stayed at it for the
rest of his life, leaving monuments and guideposts for subsequent seekers like us.

Searching for the mind of the Church meant searching
for her spokesmen—not just anyone with an opinion about
the Bible, that is, but for ambassadors duly authorized. By
Clement's time, this meant a search for *the disciples of the disciples.* The original Twelve, writes Eusebius, had **"already
fulfilled the command of the Saviour, and had distributed
their goods to the needy. Then starting out upon long
journeys they performed the office of evangelists, being
filled with the desire to preach Christ to those who had
not yet heard the word of faith."** Later, having **"only laid
the foundations of the faith in foreign places, they appointed others as pastors, and entrusted them with the
nurture of those that had recently been brought in, while
they themselves went on again to other countries and nations, with the grace and the co-operation of God."**[2] Eusebius names Quadratus as one of these immediate successors,
whom he identifies as one of the seventy disciples sent out

---

[2] Eusebius, *Church History*, bk. 3, chap. 37: www.newadvent.org/fathers/
250103.htm.

by the Lord in Luke 10; also Ignatius and Clement of Rome, so prominent in our story already. Polycarp is mentioned as well, disciple of St. John at Smyrna, who was martyred while Clement was just a child. Clement and Justin would have got on like a house afire, no doubt, both of them being adult converts from Greek philosophy; but Justin, too, likely earned his martyr's reward before Clement's search ever got started. Any other potential stops on his itinerary are guess-work. Certainly Irenaeus was flourishing in the 180s; but he was serving as a missionary on the far western frontier of Gaul. There is some surviving evidence that Clement met Tatian, Justin's own disciple at Rome, but this at a time when Tatian had begun to dally, like Tertullian, with the schism of the Montanists or something very like it, and, as such, would have been little use to a man like Clement of Athens, seeking the mind of the vast orthodox majority.

One lead, however, appears to have captured Clement's imagination like nothing else. He heard about the daring missionary Pantaenus, now ensconced as the head of a great underground school for Christians—the first-ever Christian *seminary*, it seems—at the empire's intellectual capital of Alexandria in Egypt. Sicilian by birth, he converted to Christ after having been an adherent of the Stoic philosophy; but Pantaenus was no idle intellectual. He had proved, in Clement's eyes, the vigor and authenticity of his faith by hard labor in a singularly unpromising field. **"They say"**, writes Eusebius, **"that he displayed such zeal for the divine Word that he was appointed as a herald of the Gospel of Christ to the nations in the East, and was sent as far as India. For indeed there were still many evangelists of the Word who sought earnestly to use their inspired zeal, after**

the examples of the apostles, for the increase and building
up of the Divine Word." And the tales Pantaenus brought
back from India were wonderful, indeed. Upon reaching
his destination, for instance, he learned to his delight that
the holy name of Jesus was not completely unknown there:
**"It is reported that among persons there who knew of
Christ, he found the Gospel according to Matthew, which
had anticipated his own arrival. For Bartholomew, one of
the apostles, had preached to them, and left with them
the writing of Matthew in the Hebrew language, which
they had preserved till that time."[3]**

When, about the year 180, Pantaenus returned to "civi-
lization" (i.e., the Roman Empire), he was persuaded to take
up his post as headmaster for the Catechetical School,[4] an
institution that, unlike modern seminaries, appears to have
included more basic lessons for laypeople as well as advanced study for scholars and prospective clergy. Jerome,
among others, tells us that the Church at Alexandria was
planted by the Evangelist Mark during one of his own first-
century missionary journeys and that the storied Catechetical School had its roots in that era; actually founded, that is,

---

[3] Eusebius, *Church History*, bk. 5, chap. 10: www.newadvent.org/fathers/
250105.htm. Many scholars have long believed that our existing Greek
Matthew is a translation or adaptation of a lost original, composed by the
Apostle in Hebrew.

[4] "The word *katechesis* means instruction by word of mouth, especially
by questioning and answering. Though it may apply to any subject-matter,
it is commonly used for instruction in the elements of religion, especially
preparation for initiation into Christianity. The word and others of the
same origin occur in St. Luke's Gospel: 'That thou mayest know the verity
of those things in which thou hast been instructed' (*katechethes*, in quibus
eruditus es—i, 4)": www.newadvent.org/cathen/05075b.htm.

during apostolic times. Even more astounding, perhaps: there are hints that the school may have predated the Church! The seminary at Alexandria, in other words, may actually have been *a school that converted*—a preexisting center of Jewish faith and learning that, having heard the message of Christ as it was originally preached, accepted that message and just kept going. (But more on this as our story continues. . . .)

No wonder Clement, after interviewing so many potential mentors, arrived at Alexandria and stopped. **"When I came upon the last [of these] (he was the first in power) having tracked him out concealed in Egypt, I found rest"**, Clement writes of Pantaenus. **"He, the true, the Sicilian bee, gathering the spoil of the flowers of the prophetic and apostolic meadow, engendered in the souls of his hearers a deathless element of knowledge."[5]** Indeed, it would seem hard to imagine a sounder chain of transmission: a heroic teacher, at a school founded for that very purpose, with deep roots in Old Testament wisdom, established under the auspices of one of the actual New Testament authors, an intimate disciple of Peter himself. The Sicilian bee, in short, was sitting atop a virtual hive of apostolic deposit— and to a man like Clement of Athens, searching for the mind of Christ, the news must have been like the first whiff of springtime honey in the nostrils of a hungry bear.

All Greek to Me

Most Christians realize that the books of the New Testament were originally written and circulated in *Greek*, the

---

[5] Clement, *Stromata* 1,1,11.

language of literacy all across the Roman Empire. Most have heard, too, that this was done so that the message of Christ might spread quickly, reaching as many potential converts as possible. All this is true as far as it goes, but there is another aspect of the story less frequently commented upon: to wit, that the Gospels and other apostolic writings contain nearly three hundred word-for-word quotations from a book that was already famous, already familiar to philosophers and other spiritual seekers, and beloved by millions of faithful God-fearers from one end of the empire to the other. That book was the Greek-language Bible called the *Septuagint*, a translation of the Hebrew Old Testament ordered up by Ptolemy II of Egypt for use by non-Jewish readers that had already enjoyed a wide circulation for *more than two hundred years* by the time the sun came up on the first Christmas morning. There is, in other words, every reason to believe that the Evangelists were aware of this huge pre-sold readership and, indeed, had these people chiefly in mind as they wrote. The third Gospel, for instance, is generally conceded to have been written with Gentile readers in view; yet it only takes a short perusal of the book to realize that it would still, despite Luke's many accommodations, be largely unintelligible to someone approaching it without any knowledge of the Old Testament at all. Thanks to the Septuagint, Luke and the other Gospel writers were able to count on that knowledge being there in advance. In this sense, the Greek New Testament may be seen as a consciously intended *sequel* or follow-up to an already booming popular success.

When Clement came to Alexandria, he entered pretty much the worldwide headquarters for those God-fearers (or *metuentes*) we mentioned. It is estimated that by his day,

Roman Egypt contained at least half a million of these semi-proselytes, or "Near Jews", as they were often called. These were men and women of Gentile ancestry who had not actually converted to Judaism but had, nevertheless, been drawn to various aspects of the Hebrew faith by means of their regular contact with the Greek-speaking, culturally Roman Jews of the Diaspora—including, of course, exposure to their fascinating religious text, the Septuagint. These dispersed or "Hellenized" Jews had, most of them, never actually set foot in their distant motherland or had any contact with the Temple sacrifices; in fact, they had adopted, due largely to necessity, an abridged, less law-heavy version of the Hebrew faith that was in many ways truer to the spirit of the original than the rabbinical Talmudism that arose under the Pharisees. They were more missionary minded, less inclined to stress the tithing of mint and dill above weightier matters, and—if their most famous exemplar, the historian Josephus, is any indication—far more friendly toward Christianity. Between them, at any rate, these two groups constituted the majority of world Judaism by the time of the Apostles, outnumbering the more familiar Holy Land Jews by a margin of perhaps five to one. And their unique combination of open hearts and preexisting familiarity with the Old Testament and its many messianic prophecies made them, by far, the population most receptive to the Gospel message on earth.

Studies have shown, in fact, that the cities where Christian growth was most explosive in these early centuries were precisely those with the largest pre-Christian populations of semi-proselytes and dispersed Jews—and chief among these was Alexandria. Another famous Jew of the Dispersion,

Philo of Alexandria, whose life on earth overlapped that of our Lord Himself, found and reported a colony of what can only be described as *monks* living there in the middle of the first century (Philo died in A.D. 50). Eusebius believed that these were very early Christians, perhaps the first fruits of St. Mark's mission in Egypt.

> **In the work to which he gave the title, *On a Contemplative Life or on Suppliants*, . . . [Philo] says that these men were called Therapeutæ, . . . explaining it from the fact that they applied remedies and healed the souls of those who came to them, by relieving them like physicians, of evil passions. . . . Whether Philo himself gave them this name, employing an epithet well suited to their mode of life, or whether the first of them really called themselves so in the beginning, since the name of Christians was not yet everywhere known, we need not discuss here. . . . The race particularly abounds in Egypt, in each of its so-called *nomes*,[6] and especially about Alexandria.**

In describing their life-style and practices, Philo

> **bears witness that first of all they renounce their property . . . [just as] it is recorded that all the companions of the apostles sold their possessions and their property and distributed to all according to the necessity of each one, so that no one among them was in want. . . .[7] He speaks as follows concerning their churches, which were scattered about here and there: In each house there is a sacred apartment which is called a sanctuary and monastery, where, quite alone,**

---

[6] A nome was one of the thirty-six territorial divisions of ancient Egypt.

[7] Cf. Acts 2:44–45.

they perform the mysteries of the religious life.[8] They
bring nothing into it, neither drink nor food, nor any
of the other things which contribute to the necessi-
ties of the body, but only the laws, and the inspired
oracles of the prophets, and hymns and such other
things as augment and make perfect their knowledge
and piety. . . . These they use as models, and imi-
tate their principles. . . . It is highly probable that the
works of the ancients, which he says they had, were the
Gospels and the writings of the apostles, and probably some expositions of the ancient prophets, such as
are contained in the Epistle to the Hebrews, and in
many others of Paul's Epistles.[9]

These *Therapeutæ*, Eusebius writes (still summarizing Philo),

not only spend their time in meditation, but they also
compose songs and hymns to God in every variety
of metre and melody, though they divide them, of
course, into measures of more than common solem-
nity. . . . Some, in whom a great desire for knowledge
dwells, forget to take food for three days; and some

---

[8] The word *mysterion* was used by the Romans to refer to ceremonial
rites of initiation; not just to various religious cults such as Mithraism, but
also to the Roman army. St. Paul uses the same word in 1 Corinthians
4:1 when he speaks of himself and his fellow Apostles as "stewards of the
mysteries of God". The word is usually translated into English by way of
the Latin, by which it becomes "sacraments". Eusebius intends to imply
that these mysteries celebrated by the Therapeutæ were already those of
the Christian Church—but it is possible that they had quasi-Christian
ceremonies of their own that predated Christianity.

[9] Eusebius says that St. Mark brought his Gospel with him on his mission to Egypt; and if that is true, then the Second Gospel may be, as some
scholars have guessed, a translation of that same Hebrew Matthew that
Bartholomew took to India, abridged for use on a Greek-speaking mission
field.

are so delighted and feast so luxuriously upon wisdom, which furnishes doctrines richly and without
stint, that they abstain even twice as long as this, and
are accustomed, after six days, scarcely to take necessary food. . . . They say that there were women also
with those of whom we are speaking, and that the
most of them were aged virgins who had preserved
their chastity, not out of necessity, as some of the
priestesses among the Greeks, but rather by their own
choice, through zeal and a desire for wisdom. . . . In
addition to this Philo describes the order of digni-
ties which exists among those who carry on the services of the church, mentioning the diaconate, and
the office of bishop, which takes the precedence over
all the others. . . . These things the above-mentioned
author has related in his own work, indicating a mode
of life which has been preserved to the present time by
us alone, recording especially the vigils kept in connection with the great festival,[10] and the exercises
performed during those vigils, and the hymns cus-
tomarily recited by us, and describing how, while one
sings regularly in time, the others listen in silence,
and join in chanting only the close of the hymns; and
how, on the days referred to they sleep on the ground
on beds of straw, and to use his own words, taste no
wine at all, nor any flesh, but water is their only drink,
and the relish with their bread is salt and hyssop.[11]

Eusebius, from his vantage point in 325, insists very em-
phatically that this combination of devotional and ascetical

---

[10] A reference to the Paschal feast of the Resurrection.

[11] Eusebius, *Church History*, bk. 2, chap. 17: www.newadvent.org/fathers/
250102.htm.

marks is **"to be found nowhere else than in the evangelical religion of the Christians"** and that Philo, **"when he wrote these things, had in view the first heralds of the Gospel and the customs handed down from the beginning by the apostles."** The discovery of the Dead Sea Scrolls, however (already lost at least two hundred years before Eusebius' day), has taught us not to jump so quickly to his conclusion. These documents, among other considerations, have revealed so much more about the many other forms of "alternative"—dare we say *quasi-Christian?*—Judaism that existed in the centuries immediately before and after the coming of Christ that our range of options for explaining Philo's *Therapeutæ* has become much broader. Curious groups such as the Essenes, for instance—who lived without money, devoted themselves to acts of charity, waited eagerly for a coming Messiah, and were led by a celibate order of elders— have caused the lines between Hellenized Jew, "Near Jew", and Jewish Christian (still very much the majority of the Church, even in the second century) to become very fine indeed.[12] Philo may have been describing a colony of Hellenized Jews so in tune with the great changes to come— "looking", like Simeon in Luke's Gospel, "for the consolation of Israel"—that they were already half-converted before they actually heard the name of the Lord's Christ. St. Mark may have arrived after Philo's report was made, found a preexisting community of Essenes thriving at Alexandria, and received them easily into the Church.

---

[12] Be that as it may, Eusebius' list of "Christian distinctives" certainly does tell us quite a lot about which practices could be considered normal Christian devotion during these early centuries.

This explains what was meant earlier about "the school that converted". Eusebius also records **"the philosophical mode of life"** Philo found among these *Therapeutæ* of Egypt:

> **The whole interval, from morning to evening, is for them a time of exercise. For they read the holy Scriptures, and explain the philosophy of their fathers in an allegorical manner, regarding the written words as symbols of hidden truth which is communicated in obscure figures. . . . For the whole law seems to these men to resemble a living organism, of which the spoken words constitute the body, while the hidden sense stored up within the words constitutes the soul. . . . They have also writings of ancient men, who were the founders of their sect, and who left many monuments of the allegorical method. These they use as models, and imitate their principles.** [13]

This allegorical approach to interpreting the Old Testament —the most familiar example of which may be our customary reading of the Bible's erotic love poem, the *Song of Solomon*, as an extended metaphor of the love between Christ and His Church—actually became the distinctive mark of Alexandrian theology in the centuries ahead; so much so that theologians frequently call it "the Alexandrian method" even today. With these facts in mind, it seems very easy, indeed, to imagine that a preexisting school of Essenes, Hellenized proselytes, or other "proto-Christians", as it were, gradually morphed into—or even suddenly "saw the light" to become—the famous Catechetical School to which Clement of Athens finally became heir.

---

[13] Eusebius, *Church History*, bk. 2, chap. 17.

By the time Eusebius was able to look back on all this, the entire phenomenon of Hellenized/Near-Judaism had vanished from the scene; the only Jews who remained in Egypt were of the modern Talmudist variety—decided Jesus-rejecters, that is. Where had the others gone? More and more, scholars are beginning to realize that practically all of them must have been caught up eventually into the victory of the Church; where, as St. Paul (writing in Greek) proclaimed, **"there cannot be Greek and Jew, circumcised and uncircumcised, barbarian, Scythian, slave, free man, but Christ is all, and in all"** (Col 3:11). Alexandria had become the great melting pot where all of these distinctions were finally amalgamated.

All this not only explains why the New Testament authors wrote in Greek but why early Christianity itself—a movement begun by Aramaic speakers raised in the Hebrew religion—came to be so overwhelmingly Greek. Not only did the early Church canonize, finally, and revere a finished New Testament of exclusively Greek documents, she continued to use the Septuagint as her Old Testament, almost exclusively. This fact is still reflected today in the bigger Bibles used by the older, liturgical communions; Bibles that, like the Septuagint itself, contain the seven deuterocanonical books often disparaged by Protestant bodies as "apocrypha".[14] Practically all of the earliest Fathers can be shown to have accepted these books as the authentic Word of God, including Irenaeus (who explicitly cites the books of Baruch

---

[14] Most Anglican Bibles do still contain the deuterocanonical books—though usually segregated from the rest as "apocrypha" (without definitely asserting that they lack divine inspiration).

and Wisdom as "Scripture") and three of the four profiled in this current volume—Clement, Origen, and Hippolytus —all of whom were, not coincidentally, educated and discipled here at Pantaenus' Catechetical School at Alexandria.[15]

Apologies to Theologies

Over more than a decade's time in Egypt, during which Pantaenus **"expounded the treasures of divine doctrine both orally and in writing"**, Clement of Athens gradually became Clement of Alexandria; studying under, collaborating with, and then finally succeeding his master as head of the Catechetical School, probably just before the turn of the third century (A.D. 200). And though the school had always, in Eusebius' words, been **"managed by men of great ability and zeal for divine things"**,[16] Clement's leadership took it to new heights, opening a whole new stage in the Church's intellectual development. "Towards 200 A.D.," as Quasten

---

[15] "Clement [of Alexandria], in his writings, affirms in the strongest possible language the inspiration and scriptural status of the Deuterocanon. . . . He quotes nearly every Deuterocanonical book at one time or another and calls them 'Scripture' in so many words. . . . The strongest proof of Origen's full acceptance of the Deuterocanon is to be found in the manner in which he employed them. . . . Origen quotes Wisdom as the word of God . . . and calls the Book of Sirach 'Holy Scripture' . . . and 'the divine word'. . . . Baruch is cited with the formula 'It is written' and used without qualification. . . . Hippolytus makes no distinction between Protocanonical and Deuterocanonical books, often quoting from both groups without qualification or distinction. In his treatise *Against Noetus*, he explicitly refers to the book of Baruch as 'Scripture.'" Gary Michuta, *Why Catholic Bibles Are Bigger* (El Cajon, Calif.: Catholic Answers Press, 2017).

[16] Both quotes from Eusebius, *Church History*, bk. 5.

writes, "ecclesiastical literature not only shows signs of tremendous growth, it takes an entirely new turn."[17]

Up to this point, the preserved writings of the early Fathers are almost entirely *defensive*; written, that is, to repel arguments against the Church's mission made by heathen persecutors, apologists for the existing pagan religions, or by splinter groups and heretics that had arisen within her own ranks. Justin Martyr, Athenagoras, Melito, Minucius Felix, even Tertullian are all examples of second-century Christian apologists "putting out fires" of one type or another. Like the New Testament itself, made up largely of letters occasioned by some pressing local need and only incidentally revealing any carefully worked out dogmas, the literary remains of these earliest Fathers contain little to no effort at theology proper. "No Christian author had as yet attempted to consider the entire body of belief as a whole or make a systematic presentation of it. Even the accomplishment of St. Irenaeus, however great its merits, does not answer the question whether ecclesiastical literature should simply remain a weapon against enemies or become a tool of peaceful work within the Church's own borders."[18]

Catechetics there always had been, of course; adult converts were always required to make a profession of faith before baptism,[19] and we do have evidence of short documents

---

[17] Johannes Quasten, *Patrology* (Allen, Tex.: Christian Classics, 1986), 2:1.

[18] Ibid.

[19] "There are very suggestive traces in the New Testament of the recognition of a certain 'form of doctrine' (*typos didaches*, Romans 6:17) which moulded, as it were, the faith of new converts to Christ's law, and which involved not only the word of faith believed in the heart, but 'with the

prepared for this purpose. The well-known Apostles' Creed is, in fact, probably one of these; it certainly represents, at any rate, a list of basic doctrines that anyone seeking communion with the apostolic churches was supposed to have learned and committed himself to. Tertullian preserves the earliest recorded version in his *De Praescriptione* (ca. 198):

> **I believe in one God, maker of the world, the Word, called His Son, Jesus Christ, by the Spirit and power of God the Father made flesh in Mary's womb, and born of her; fastened to a cross. He rose the third day, was caught up into heaven, and set at the right hand of the Father, [He] will come with glory to take the good into life eternal, and condemn the wicked to perpetual fire, [He] sent the vicarious power of His Holy Spirit, to govern believers; [I believe in the] restoration of the flesh.[20]**

It did not, however, take a whole school to teach these short articles (in fact, some form of the Apostles' Creed was probably taught in every local church throughout the world), so even the basic curriculum at Alexandria must have included a good deal more than the very basics.

All the same, Clement's term as rector is generally marked as a real watershed. This seems to have been the moment

---

mouth confession made unto salvation' (Romans 10:8–10). In close connection with this we must recall the profession of faith in Jesus Christ exacted of the eunuch (Acts 8:37) as a preliminary to baptism (Augustine, 'De Fide et Operibus', cap. ix; Migne, P.L., LVII, 205) and the formula of baptism itself in the name of the Three Persons of the Blessed Trinity (Matthew 28:19; and cf. the Didache 7:2, and 9:5)." See "Apostles' Creed", *CE*.

[20] Quoted in "Apostles' Creed", in *CE*: www.newadvent.org/cath en/o16 29a.htm.

where the Church's mind progressed *from apologies to theologies*: "The deeper the new religion penetrated the ancient world, the more the need was felt for an exposition of its tenets that was orderly, comprehensive and exact. The more numerous the converts in educated circles, the greater the necessity to give such catechumens an instruction corresponding to their environment and to train teachers for that purpose." Clement's whole life could now be seen as a long preparation to become a new kind of missionary—an evangelist to the erudite.

> [He] knew very well that the Church could not avoid competition with pagan philosophy and literature if she was to fulfill her duty towards mankind and live up to her task as teacher of the nations. His Hellenistic education enabled him to make of the Christian faith a system of thought with a scientific foundation. We owe it above all to him if scholarly thinking and research are recognized in the Church. He proved that the faith and philosophy, Gospel and secular learning, are not enemies but belong together. All secular learning serves theology. Christianity is the crown and glory of all the truths that are found in the various philosophical doctrines.[21]

If Pantaenus was a literary man, none of his books have survived; Clement, on the other hand, left us four, the first three of which make up a kind of trilogy. All four of them fully demonstrate both the breathtaking depth of his education and the breadth of his interests and sympathies. Clement had a good working knowledge of poetry, science,

---

[21] Quasten, *Patrology*, 2:1, 6–7.

philosophy—even archaeology. Scholars have also guessed that he got full use out of his Alexandrian Library card as well. Yes, that great lost library of antiquity was still standing proud in Clement's day, and his books are chock-a-block with direct quotations from pagan authors such as Epimenides, Menander, and Euripides (a practice that was pioneered, recall, by the Apostle Paul himself).[22] In fact, it is due to Clement's love for these authors and his penchant for quotation that at least a few fragments of many otherwise lost philosophical works have been preserved. His familiarity with early Christian literature, however, is where Clement really shines. Where our friend Hermas, God love him, hardly knows the Bible at all, Clement quotes or alludes to the Greek Old Testament more than a thousand times and references the New in nearly two thousand places. He also knows the writings of the earlier Fathers (not many of those!) and keeps a broad catalogue of heretical quotes on hand as well (mostly Gnostic and Marcionite)—along with ready refutations for the errors they contain.

The first of the trilogy is *Protreptikos pros Ellenas*—a title usually translated as *The Exhortation to the Greeks*. This book is a straight-up Gospel tract aimed at educated pagans—but what a tract! "The discourse opens with passages which fall on the ear with the effect of sweet music. Amphion and Arion by their minstrelsy drew after them savage monsters and moved the very stones; but Christ is the noblest minstrel. His harp and lyre are men. He draws music from their hearts by the Holy Spirit: nay, Christ is Himself the New Canticle, whose melody subdues the fiercest and hardest

---

[22] Cf. Acts 17:28; Rom 7:19; Titus 1:12.

natures."[23] He encourages his readers to believe that God has been leading them already, even in their study of pagan literature—a process that needs purification, of course, and exposure to the new facts supplied by inspired Scripture, but not simply renunciation. Though he mercilessly skewers many aspects of popular pagan religion, his purpose is to draw his readers "farther up and farther in", until they reach the heart of true philosophy that is found in the Christian religion. Clement also defends philosophy against the objection that it is of no value to Christians. He answers that philosophy is given by God and was granted to the Greeks by divine providence in the same way as the Law to the Jews. "Before the advent of the Lord, philosophy was . . . a kind of preparatory training to those who [would later] attain to faith through demonstration."[24] Clement finishes his exhortation with a direct appeal: **"What, then, is the exhortation I give you? I urge you to be saved. This Christ desires. In one word, He freely bestows life on you. And who is He? Briefly learn. The Word of truth, the Word of incorruption that generates man by bringing him back to the truth — the goad that urges to salvation — He who expels destruction and pursues death — He who builds up the temple of God in men that He may cause God to take up His abode in men."[25]**

If the *Exhortation* was meant to draw sinners to the baptismal font, the second book in the trilogy is spiritual boot

---

[23] "Clement", in *CE*: www.newadvent.org/cathen/04045a.htm.

[24] Clement, *The Stromata*, bk. 1, chap. 5. www.newadvent.org/fathers/021 01.htm.

[25] Clement, *Exhortation*, chap. 11: www.earlychristianwritings.com/text/clement-exhortation.html.

camp for new recruits. Those who may have wondered if
Clement was being too soft on heathenism in the first volume got perhaps more balance than they were bargaining
for in these pages, for *The Instructor* is nothing less than
a round of *detox* for those coming fresh out of the pagan
life-style. Though the tone of the book is kindly and understanding (Clement was, after all, a convert himself), he
prescribes here a demanding regimen by which newbies,
coming into the Church muddied and bloodied by all the
horrors of a previous life without God, may **"[escape] the
defilements of the world"** (2 Pet 2:20). The Logos Himself
is the Instructor, the spirit of Christ working to transmute
and transform; **"His aim"**, at this point, **"is to improve the
soul, not to teach, and to train it up to a virtuous, not
to an intellectual life."**[26] Theology, in other words, will
come later—milk rather than meat is needed at this stage.
"Nothing is too common or trivial for the Tutor's care. His
influence tells on the minute details of life, on one's manner of eating, drinking, sleeping, dressing, taking recreation,
etc."[27]—though, to head off a misunderstanding, not all of
these regulations were intended for life outside boot camp,
for all ordinary Christians everywhere, that is. And despite
the book's high, strenuous moral tone, it is quite apparent that Clement himself was no babe in the woods; whole
chapters of *The Instructor*, detailing practical ways to "come
down" from addictions to the second-century equivalent
of sex, drugs, and rock 'n' roll, were so frank and shocking
to nineteenth-century readers that the translators of at least

---

[26] Clement, *Instructor*, I,1,1,4: www.newadvent.org/fathers/02091.htm.
[27] "Clement", in *CE*.

one well-known English edition opted simply to leave them in Latin, in order to dissuade idle curiosity.[28]

The final book of the three was abandoned by its author in an unfinished state. If the *Exhortation* was a call to initial belief and the *Instructor* a program of preparatory discipline, *The Teacher* (as we believed he intended to call it) was to be the reward for perseverance; the meat to the milk, an initiation into fullness of truth. Here, at last, was where Clement hoped to display his mature system of carefully thought out, interconnected Christian theology—but he appears to have been interrupted mysteriously by some disruptive circumstance. Returning later to the half-finished work and finding it to be not much more than a collection of notes and sketches for a project far too ambitious to complete under the changed conditions, Clement apparently decided to punt, as it were. He opted to publish the incomplete version in its "as is" condition, dubbing it his *Stromata* (an apt title, which is sometimes translated as "The Patchwork Quilt"), and adding only a brief recognition of its disordered state. And it really is something of a mess—but a grand one, to be sure. The introduction has either been lost or was never written at all; and the final section actually led Clement to be accused of heresy after his death!—until scholars finally recognized it as nothing more than a grab bag of excerpts from pagan philosophers, probably collected at the Library of Alexandria; an appendix at the most, if it was ever meant to be included to begin with.

Nevertheless, Clement's *Stromateis* is his most magnificent

---

[28] Though *The Instructor* was written in Greek, the best surviving manuscript is an old Latin translation.

work. He begins by defending once more (against overly cautious critics within his own communion, it seems) the use of non-Christian science and philosophy to illumine Christian subjects. One of the ways he hopes to allay such concerns is to defend the concept of *faith* against the common pagan charge that it represents only an irrational leap in the dark, blind adherence to superstitions that lack any real basis: **"Faith, which the Greeks disparage, deeming it futile and barbarous, is a voluntary preconception, the assent of piety — 'the subject of things hoped for, the evidence of things not seen' [Heb 11:1] according to the divine apostle.**[29] **. . . Without faith it is impossible to please God."**[30] Philosophy, in other words, can never take the place of divine revelation but must only act as a supplement to it. To underscore this idea dramatically, Clement reasserts Justin Martyr's still-recent contention that Plato and others of the earlier philosophers were familiar with the Torah even before the Septuagint appeared—and actually cribbed many of their best ideas from Moses!

Most important for our purpose in these pages, however, is Clement's Christian prophylactic against the adulteration of our beliefs through all this contact with paganism. How can believers assure themselves that the original faith **"which was once for all delivered to the saints"** [Jude 3] is not being slowly, imperceptibly transmogrified by this

---

[29] This phrase is notable as a very early example of a knowledgeable scholar attributing the book of Hebrews to St. Paul (in at least some sense).

[30] Clement, *Stromata*, bk. 2, chap. 2, in *Ante-Nicene Fathers*, vol. 2, ed. Alexander Roberts and James Donaldson (1885; Peabody, Mass.: Hendrickson, 1995), p. 349.

openness and so-called liberality? Did the Apostle Paul not warn that **"that you must no longer walk as the Gentiles walk, in the futility of their minds"** [Eph 4:17]? Had the Apostle James not cautioned that **"whoever wishes to be a friend of the world makes himself an enemy of God"** [Jas 4:4]? Had he not spoken, as well, against a wisdom that **"descendeth not from above, but is earthly, sensual, devilish"** [Jas 3:15 KJV]? Perhaps it really is an ugly thing to hole up in one's cabin, to be called backward and insular, in order to avoid all possibility of contamination; but if the only alternative is to risk St. John's censure—that **"if any one loves the world, love for the Father is not in him"** [1 Jn 2:15]—then perhaps we ought not to take any chances? Clement of Alexandria's second-century answers to these still perfectly valid questions are carefully and decisively outlined in the last few chapters of the *Stromata*—his trilogy's big finale.

One Royal Highway

First of all, Clement's school was *a Bible school*. As strongly as any second-millennium fundamentalist, he asserts the inspiration and infallibility of the Holy Scriptures. However convinced we may be of the value of human reason, Clement insists that **"He who believes . . . the divine Scriptures with sure judgment, receives in the voice of God, who bestowed the Scripture, a demonstration that cannot be impugned. Faith, then, is not established by** [philosophical] **demonstration"**, but only by consulting the Divine Word; **" 'Blessed therefore' "**, he adds, invoking the memory of Christ to doubting Thomas, are **" 'those who, not having**

seen, yet have believed' [Jn 20:29]."[31] We try to understand as much of our religion as we can through rational
thought processes; the rest we accept on trust until we *can*
understand it. Either way, **"those who are ready to toil in
the most excellent pursuits, will not desist from the search
after truth, till they get the demonstration from the Scriptures themselves."** As we noted in connection with Hermas
and his Shepherd, the books of the Bible gained their great
authority because of their origin; because, that is, of who
gave them—and we discover who gave them by establishing
to *whom* they were given. **"For we have, as the source of
teaching, the Lord, both by the prophets, the Gospel, and
the blessed apostles"** (in both Old and New Testaments,
that is) 'in various manners and at sundry times,' [Heb 1:1]
leading from the beginning of knowledge to the end. . . .
[In this manner] **we are by the voice of the Lord trained
up to the knowledge of the truth. . . . Accordingly, those
fall from this eminence who follow not God whither He
leads. And He leads us in the inspired Scriptures."**

"We may not", Clement insists, **"give our adhesion to
men on a bare statement by them, who might equally state
the opposite . . . but we establish the matter that is in
question by the voice of the Lord."**[32] Yet this was never
Sola Scriptura as popular Protestantism conceives it.[33] With-

---

[31] Clement, *Stromata*, bk. 2, chap. 2: www.newadvent.org/fathers/02102
.htm.

[32] Clement, *Stromata*, bk. 7, chap. 16.

[33] *Sola Scriptura* (Scripture alone) is the belief that the Bible alone is
sufficient as our sole rule of faith, and thus no creed or tradition of the
Church can be considered authoritative. "Material sufficiency", on the
other hand, is the conviction that all Christian doctrines can be found in

out an interpreter, the Scriptures are silent, for to be really *sola*, they must sit on the shelf alone, unread. Even the private individual, working unaided, interprets what he is reading and may do it well or poorly. Those who attempt this method eventually **"despise and laugh at one another. And it happens that the same thought is held in the highest estimation by some, and by others condemned for insanity."**[34]

The commonly heard assertion that "the Bible interprets itself" was actually taught by Clement in the 190s: **"[T]he truth is not found by changing the meanings"** of words or by taking them out of context, **"(for so people subvert all true teaching), but in the consideration of what perfectly belongs to and becomes the Sovereign God, and in establishing each one of the points demonstrated in the Scriptures again from similar Scriptures."**[35] The avowal, then, that Scripture interprets itself is essentially true—the question is *to whom* does it interpret itself? How do we know which workman has done this work of comparison correctly? Those groups that most strongly claim to be using this method differ among themselves in the final result to practically the same degree as private individuals. Clement, as we are about to see, understood very well that even a book divinely inspired needs some additional

---

Holy Scripture, either explicitly or implicitly, or are deducible from it." This material sufficiency was and is the belief of the apostolic Church. All who accept *sola Scriptura* believe in material sufficiency, but not *vice versa* —a missed distinction that often causes unnecessary confusion in regard to this topic.

[34] Clement, *Stromata*, bk. 7, chap. 16.

[35] Ibid.

authority besides itself if it is ever to act as the arbiter *between* interpreters, however well meaning.

"It is possible", as our friend (and Clement's contemporary) Irenaeus has already taught us, **"for everyone in every Church, who may wish to know the truth, to contemplate the tradition of the Apostles which has been made known throughout the world . . .** [for the Apostles] **wished . . . their successors to be perfect and without reproach, to whom they handed on their authority."**[36] In the writings of the Fathers, Scripture and tradition are both part of the same authoritative deposit, since they both originate from the same source: that group of carefully schooled disciples, that is, to whom the Savior said: **"He who hears you hears me, and he who rejects you rejects me, and he who rejects me rejects him who sent me"** (Lk 10:16). Clement picks up this theme in the *Stromata* when he comes to address the stumbling block to conversions posed by the rise of heretical sects: **"As those almonds are called empty in which the contents are worthless, not those in which there is nothing; so also we call those heretics empty, who are destitute of the counsels of God and the traditions of Christ; bitter, in truth, like the wild almond, their dogmas originating with themselves . . . we must never, as do those who follow the heresies, adulterate the truth, or steal the canon** [literally, *the measuring stick*] **of the Church."**

A genuinely spiritual disciple, as Clement continues, **"having grown old in the Scriptures, and maintaining apostolic and ecclesiastic orthodoxy in doctrines, lives most correctly in accordance with the Gospel, and discovers the**

---

[36] *FEF* 1:89, no. 209.

proofs, for which he may have made search . . . from the law and the prophets. For the life of [such a person], in my view, is nothing but deeds and words corresponding to the tradition of the Lord." Tradition, in this sense, does not extract from Scripture anything that was not already there, but only uncovers the true meaning of what was present all along. "The knowledge of the truth among us from what is already believed, produces faith in what is not yet believed."[37]

How can we show that these "apostolic traditions" really are apostolic? Just as we saw Irenaeus and Justin doing in *Four Witnesses*, Clement proves it by demonstrating that heretical disunity is *a recent development*, while the cohesive tradition of the Church predates the advent of the dissident splinter groups by many years: "For that the human assemblies which they held were posterior to the Catholic Church requires not many words to show. For the teaching of our Lord at His advent, beginning with Augustus and Tiberius, was completed in the middle of the times of Tiberius [who ruled from A.D. 14 to 37]. And that of the apostles, embracing the ministry of Paul, ends with Nero [whose rule was 54 to 68]. It was later, in the times of Adrian the king [Roman emperor from 117 to 138], that those who invented the heresies arose."[38]

What [Clement asks,] remained to be said—in ecclesiastical knowledge I mean—by such men [as] Marcion, for example, [born in 85] or Prodicus [an obscure heretic of the mid-second century], and such like, who

---

[37] Clement, *Stromata*, bk. 7, chap. 16.
[38] Ibid., chap. 17.

> did not walk in the right way? For they could not have
> surpassed their predecessors in wisdom, so as to dis-
> cover anything in addition to what had been uttered
> by them; for they would have been satisfied had they
> been able to learn the things laid down before. . . .
> Such being the case, it is evident, from the high an-
> tiquity and perfect truth of the Church, that these
> later heresies, and those yet subsequent to them in
> time, were new inventions falsified [from the truth].[39]

For the Catholic Church, the apostolic traditions act as the
guardrails on the highway of faith—making them safer for
both theologians and philosophers and for ordinary reading by laypeople. Tradition is the key to confident Bible
study.[40] Not having this key, **"but a false (and as the common phrase expresses it), a counterfeit key . . . , by which
they do not enter in as we enter in, through the tradition
of the Lord,"** Clement continues, **"but bursting through
the side-door, and digging clandestinely through the wall
of the Church, and stepping over the truth"**, heretics set
themselves up as **"the Mystagogues of[41] the soul of the
impious".[42]**

**"Maintain the traditions even as I have delivered them
to you"**, wrote Paul the Apostle in 1 Corinthians 11:2; and
this practice, in Clement's eyes, is how the Church has kept

---

[39] Ibid., chap. 16.

[40] This is where the witness of the Fathers really becomes critical; their
writings can be referenced to show that the apostolic churches have not
changed their interpretation since the time of the Apostles—a verifiable
chain of custody.

[41] Mystagogues (also known as hierophants) initiated others into the se-
crets of the mystery cults.

[42] Clement, *Stromata*, bk. 7, chap. 17.

her precious and God-honoring *oneness*, standing like a beacon to the world, up till the turn of the third century. " 'The Mother draws the children to herself and we seek our Mother, the Church'[43]. . . O mystic marvel! The universal Father is one, and the universal Word; and the Holy Spirit is one and the same everywhere, and one is the only virgin mother; I love to call her the Church . . . calling her children to her, she nurses them with holy milk . . . the Word for childhood."[44]

For St. Ignatius, Christ rose from the dead so that "He might raise aloft a banner for His saints and believers in every age, whether among the Jews or among the gentiles, united in a single body in His Church."[45] For St. Irenaeus, the Church was like the Sun, "that creature of God, [which] is one and the same throughout the whole world . . . and enlightens all men that are willing to come to a knowledge of the truth." She believes and teaches her doctrine, "just as if she had but one soul, and one and the same heart, and she proclaims them, and teaches them, and hands them down, with perfect harmony, as if she possessed only one mouth. For, although the languages of the world are dissimilar, yet the import of the tradition is one and the same."[46] Likewise, Hermas' Tower of stones is one: "All the nations which dwell under heaven, when they heard and believed, were called by the name of the Son of God. When, therefore, they received the seal,

---

[43] Clement, *Instructor*, 1,5,21,1.

[44] Ibid., 1,6,42,1.

[45] *FEF* 1:24, no. 62.

[46] Irenaeus, *Against Heresies*, bk. 1, chap. 10: www.newadvent.org/fathers/0103110.htm.

they had one understanding and one mind; and their faith became one, and one their love . . . and that is why the structure of the tower was in one splendid color like the sun."[47]

Now, Clement of Alexandria writes of the "one royal highway" prepared for the faithful, though there are many other roads available, "some leading to a precipice, some to a rushing river or to a deep sea"—but the wise will "make use of the safe, and royal, and frequented way". In this way, the Christian will "distinguish what is hostile, and unseemly, and unnatural, and false, from what is true, consistent, and seemly, and according to nature. And these means must be employed in order to attain to the knowledge of the real truth."[48]

"According to my opinion", Clement writes in another passage, "the grades here in the Church, of bishops, [priests], deacons, are imitations of the angelic glory, and of that economy which, the Scriptures say, awaits those who, following the footsteps of the apostles, have lived in perfection of righteousness according to the Gospel."[49] Elsewhere, in a famous passage, he insists that

the true Church, that which is really ancient, is one, and that in it those who according to God's purpose are just, are enrolled. For from the very reason that God is one, and the Lord one, that which is in the highest degree honourable is lauded in consequence of its singleness, being an imitation of the one first principle. In the nature of the One, then, is associated

---

[47] *FEF* 1:36, no. 93.

[48] Clement, *Stromata*, bk. 7, chap. 15.

[49] Ibid., bk. 6, chap. 13: www.newadvent.org/fathers/02106.htm.

in a joint heritage the one Church, which they [the heretics] strive to cut asunder into many sects.

Therefore in substance and idea, in origin, in pre-eminence, we say that the ancient and Catholic Church is alone, collecting as it does into the unity of the one faith—which results from the peculiar Testaments, or rather the one Testament in different times by the will of the one God, through one Lord—those already ordained, whom God predestinated, knowing before the foundation of the world that they would be righteous. But the pre-eminence of the Church, as the principle of union, is, in its oneness, in this surpassing all things else, and having nothing like or equal to itself.[50]

"Let us complete the fair face of the church", Clement pleads, returning once again to his evangelistic voice, "and let us run as children to our good mother. And if we become listeners to the Word, let us glorify the blessed dispensation by which man is trained and sanctified as a child of God, and has his conversation in heaven, being trained from earth, and there receives the Father, whom he learns to know on earth. The Word both does and teaches all things, and trains in all things."[51]

Life's Legacy

The changed conditions that caused Clement to give up on *The Teacher* were probably connected to a renewed outbreak of persecution. Several early passages in the *Stromata* appear

---

[50] Ibid., bk. 7, chap. 17.
[51] Clement, *Instructor*, bk. 3, chap. 12: www.newadvent.org/fathers/02093 .htm.

to reference new laws harassing the school, beginning about 202. This, as we learn from other sources, was the start of the very serious persecution under Septimius Severus. A letter written about ten years later, by one of Clement's former students, Alexander—now bishop of Jerusalem—reveals that his mentor had been forced to flee Alexandria during that crisis. He took refuge for a while in Caesarea and became an evangelist there, ministering to suffering believers in prison and elsewhere. Another brief letter from Alexander—to Asclepiades, the new bishop of Antioch—reveals that, by 215, Clement of Alexandria was dead.

His legacy, however, not only lived, and lives on, but that legacy, by God's providence, far exceeded the fruits of his own life's work. Clement's school, as it turns out, became a veritable greenhouse for the growing of great Christian scholars and saints. Its illustrious alumni include Dionysius the Great (great opponent of the Novatian heresy); Pierius (a much-later headmaster who gave a famous sermon about the Virgin Mary); Didymus the Blind (master for fifty years during the worst of the Arian crisis); and the great theologians Peter of Alexandria and Cyril of Jerusalem.

Most notably for our purposes: Clement had been the revered personal tutor of both Hippolytus of Rome and Origen Adamantius, with whom we will be privileged to spend the remainder of the book.

Hippolytus of Rome

In the year 1551, more than thirteen centuries after the time of our witnesses, an Italian archaeologist named Pirro Ligorio discovered a battered marble statue buried near a ruined church in Rome. Though badly damaged (missing head and shoulders), it was still recognizable as the image of some venerable person seated in a chair, wearing the Greek pallium of a scholar. Guessing that it might have originally stood in a cemetery near the church, Ligorio had it extracted from the ground and cleaned for examination. He was disappointed to find that any name that may once have been inscribed had not survived—but there were inscriptions. On the curved back of the chair, a list of book titles was engraved, along with an astronomical table for calculating the date of Easter for the years 217 to 333. It did not take long for scholars to realize that these were the very books and the very table that Eusebius and Jerome, writing in the 300s, ascribed to an important but rather mysterious figure of the previous century, Hippolytus of Rome.

Though the date of his birth is unknown, Hippolytus was, according to Photius,[1] a disciple of Irenaeus of Lyons—meaning that his lifetime must have straddled the turn of the third century, the year A.D. 200. Another writer pegs him as a student at the school of Alexandria as well; the pupil, perhaps, of Clement or Pantaenus. Jerome says he

---

[1] Photius I was patriarch of Constantinople in the late ninth century.

became a bishop—but does not know where. Later Eastern writers call him not only bishop, but bishop of Rome itself —the most honored See in Christendom. Yet the Liberian Catalogue (a listing of Roman bishops dating from 354) calls Hippolytus only a priest, not a bishop, much less the pope of Rome. Eusebius, who knows so many details about Origen's life that he fills up nearly a whole book of his *Church History* with the stuff, credits Hippolytus with a similar importance —yet knows practically nothing about him, can only repeat the list of books we mentioned, and even several of those were already lost. Pope Damasus I, on the other hand (who presided during the 360s), honored the tomb of Hippoly-tus with a monument—but also mentions, almost in pass-ing, that he had been a follower of Novatian, founder of a schismatic counter-church that lasted for several centuries. Finally, the poet Prudentius (fifth century) wrote a hymn celebrating him as a martyr.

None of this adds up, does it? Was Hippolytus so fa-mous a theologian as to rank with Origen—or a figure so obscure as to be nearly forgotten just a few decades later? Was he a martyr who split with the pope—or a pope who split with the Church? Medieval scholars guessed that mul-tiple Hippolytuses might actually be involved; that what may have been several perfectly good biographies, that is, were scrambled through the years into one very bad one. Those with a taste for conspiracy theory, on the other hand, wondered if something might not have been *covered up* in all this—something prejudicial to the honor of the Roman Church. Both groups, as it happens, turned out to be wrong in the end; but it took two additional discoveries beyond the statue—in 1740 and 1851—to bring all the scattered shards together into one coherent picture.

Once we did have all the pieces in place, an amazing story came to light, a story that not only cleared up most of Hippolytus' personal history but also revealed a unique and poignant moment in Church history practically unmatched for its illustration of Christian forgiveness and redemption. And though the theology of Hippolytus is certainly worthy of the closest study, it is his value as an eyewitness to early Christian worship and sacramental beliefs that we will center on here. If Justin Martyr was our most valuable testifier in these matters the last time around—describing to Marcus Aurelius so many priceless details about a regular Sunday service, ca. 155—then Hippolytus, attacking the same problem not more than sixty years later, might be fittingly described as "Justin on steroids". When we come to examine his *Apostolike Paradosis* (*The Apostolic Tradition*), we will find descriptions of the Eucharistic prayer service, the ordination of a bishop, and the rites of baptism and confirmation that could hardly be fuller if a newsman had been present with his camera.

The Muratorian Canon

For many years, his earliest work was thought to be a *Commentary on the Book of Daniel*, written about 202. By the late nineteenth century, however, many of the best patristics scholars had come to believe Hippolytus had had a hand in the creation of the puzzling *Muratorian Canon*—a document that, even today, stands as the oldest attempt at a biblical "contents page" still in existence. If so, then our subject was a young, recently ordained presbyter with a great resume (disciple of Irenaeus!), laboring at the church of Rome as early as 180; working on the vital project of comparing biblical canons, sifting the evidence for apostolic origins, striving to help recognize the correct and final list.

Uncovered by the historian Ludovico Muratori in 1740, the document is only a fragment of a longer piece of work, and even what remains is a bad Latin translation of a Greek original in poor physical condition. Even so, it provides a priceless window into the formation of the New Testament as we know it; including, as it does, not only its very early list of candidates for inclusion but also important traditions about their origins and authorship. The beginning of the document is missing, but context suggests that an Old Testament canon may have preceded what remains. As it is, the Muratorian canon begins with **"the third book of the Gospel"**, which is **"that according to Luke"**.

"Luke, the well-known physician," writes the author of the fragment, **"after the ascension of Christ, when Paul had taken [him] with him as one zealous for the law, composed it in his own name, according to [the general] belief. Yet he himself had not seen the Lord in the flesh; and therefore, as he was able to ascertain events, so indeed he begins to tell the story from the birth of John."**[2] Next,

The fourth of the Gospels is that of John, [one] of the disciples. To his fellow disciples and bishops, who

---

[2] Luke himself confesses (1:1–4) that he was not an eyewitness to the events he records but gained his information through oral tradition and his own investigations.

had been urging him [to write], he said, "Fast with me from today to three days, and what will be revealed to each one let us tell it to one another." In the same night it was revealed to Andrew, [one] of the apostles, that John should write down all things in his own name while all of them should review it. And so, though various elements may be taught in the individual books of the Gospels, nevertheless this makes no difference to the faith of believers, since by the one sovereign Spirit all things have been declared in all [the Gospels]: concerning the nativity, concerning the passion, concerning the resurrection, concerning life with his disciples, and concerning his twofold coming; the first in lowliness when he was despised, which has taken place, the second glorious in royal power, which is still in the future. What marvel is it then, if John so consistently mentions these particular points also in his Epistles, saying about himself, "What we have seen with our eyes and heard with our ears and our hands have handled, these things we have written to you?" [1 Jn 1:1]. For in this way he professes [himself] to be not only an eye-witness and hearer, but also a writer of all the marvelous deeds of the Lord, in their order.

Moreover [continues Muratori's ancient fragment], the acts of all the apostles were written in one book. [Writing] for "most excellent Theophilus" Luke compiled the individual events that took place in his presence — as he plainly shows by omitting the martyrdom of Peter as well as the departure of Paul from the city [of Rome] when he journeyed to Spain.[3]

---

[3] Both of these extra-biblical occurrences took place after the book of Acts had already been completed.

As for the Epistles of Paul, they themselves make
clear to those desiring to understand, which ones
[they are], from what place, or for what reason they
were sent. First of all, to the Corinthians, prohibiting
their heretical schisms; next, to the Galatians, against
circumcision; then to the Romans he wrote at length,
explaining the order (or, plan) of the Scriptures, and
also that Christ is their principle (or, main theme). It is
necessary for us to discuss these one by one, since the
blessed apostle Paul himself, following the example
of his predecessor John, writes by name to only seven
churches in the following sequence: To the Corinthians first, to the Ephesians second, to the Philippians
third, to the Colossians fourth, to the Galatians fifth,
to the Thessalonians sixth, to the Romans seventh. It
is true that he writes once more to the Corinthians
and to the Thessalonians for the sake of admonition,
yet it is clearly recognizable that there is one Church
spread throughout the whole extent of the earth. For
John also in the Apocalypse, though he writes to seven
churches, nevertheless speaks to all.[4]

St. Paul wrote to individuals as well as to churches; **"out
of affection and love one to Philemon, one to Titus, and
two to Timothy; and these are held sacred in the esteem
of the Church catholic for the regulation of ecclesiastical discipline."** Here, however, the Canonist shows that he
is willing to reject as well as approve candidates for inclusion: **"There is current also [an epistle] to the Laodiceans,**

---

[4] Like St. John in the book of Revelation, St. Paul wrote seven epistles
to individual churches (a number achieved by treating Second Corinthians
and Second Thessalonians as appendices to the original letters); this perfect number seven indicates, according to several of the Fathers, that the
letters are to be thought of as addressed to the whole universal Church.

[and] another to the Alexandrians, [both] forged in Paul's name to [further] the heresy of Marcion, and several others which cannot be received into the catholic Church — for it is not fitting that gall be mixed with honey."[5] Notice that the Epistle to the Hebrews is neither accepted nor rejected by the Muratorian researcher, indicating that the jury may still have been out on that title—perhaps due to already existing doubts about its purported Pauline authorship.

As for the general epistles, the Canonist affirms that "the epistle of Jude and two of the above-mentioned (or, bearing the name of) John are counted (or, used) in the catholic [Church]" but does not mention the book of James or either of the two epistles of Peter. Since 1 Peter, at least, has been shown by other means to have gained acceptance at Rome very early on, most experts suspect that another gap in the text accounts for these omissions.

Perhaps the oddest sentence in the Muratorian fragment concerns the book of "Wisdom, written by the friends of Solomon in his honour" which our Canonist seems to wish to include in his New Testament. The Wisdom of Solomon, part of that longer Septuagint canon we discussed, was indeed used by the Fathers and considered by the early Church to be an inspired book of the Bible—but always as part of its *Old Testament*, not the New, since it was written at least fifty years prior to the coming of Christ. Here, too, the best

---

[5] Several other books get the boot quite explicitly in the fragment: "We accept nothing whatever of Arsinous or Valentinus or Miltiades, who also composed a new book of psalms for Marcion, together with Basilides, the Asian founder of the Cataphrygians."

answer to the mystery probably lies in the poor condition of the fragment.

Finally, among many other such books, **"we receive only the apocalypses of John and Peter, though some of us are not willing that the latter be read in church."**[6] As we noted earlier, the book of Revelation was accepted by the Church at Rome as early as the days of St. Clement (of Rome), though it had not yet achieved wide acceptance in the Eastern churches even by the time of Hippolytus. This other apocalypse, however, the one ascribed to Peter, was still undergoing a process of discernment as we can see here. In those days before mechanical printing, the solemn, public reading aloud before the congregation that was part of every service (a practice that the Church inherited from the synagogue) was basically the layman's only exposure to the written Word of God. A book's acceptance for such purposes, therefore—especially by one of the major churches known to have been personally founded by one of the Apostles—was practically the sign or test of its canonicity; before, that is, these final efforts were undertaken to reconcile all the minor variations Church-wide. The Canonist's unwillingness to sanction the *Apocalypse of Peter* for liturgical use (without actually condemning its contents as heretical) shows that he, and others as well, considered it to be harmless and, indeed, orthodox, but not actually inspired.

---

[6] Apocalypses are ancient books, both Jewish and Christian, that use symbolic imagery and visions of an impending cataclysm to picture God's eventual renovation of the world into a kingdom of righteousness. Pre-Christian books of this type are the *Book of Enoch* and the *Fourth Book of Esdras*; Christian examples (some heretical, some orthodox) include an *Apocalypse of Paul* and the *Apocalypse of Peter* mentioned here.

One of the best proofs that Hippolytus might be behind this Muratorian list is, in fact, his conditional acceptance of the *Apocalypse of Peter*. That book's greatest champion, as it happens, had been *Clement of Alexandria*, who even honored it by writing a commentary; and Clement seems to have passed his somewhat eccentric opinion on the subject down to later students and teachers at the Catechetical School—including, it would appear, Hippolytus of Rome.[7]

One more strange apocalyptic work gets a Muratorian glance as well: *The Shepherd of Hermas*. In reviewing his candidates, the Canonist has been looking, it seems, for books with roots in the apostolic age, in the first Christian century, that is; **"But Hermas wrote the *Shepherd* very recently, in our times, in the city of Rome, while bishop Pius, his brother, was occupying the [episcopal] chair of the church of the city of Rome [140–154]. And therefore it ought indeed to be read; but it cannot be read publicly to the people in church either among the Prophets, whose number is complete, or among the Apostles, for it is after [their] time."[8]** This is the passage we cited earlier which tried to assign Hermas' book to a date so late that its avowed connection to Clement of Rome would become impossible. As we guessed in the first chapter, however, there is no reason why a volume that earned most of its fame during Pius' era might not have been in the works for several decades before that. As for Pius I having been the "brother" of

---

[7] It is notable that Eusebius can still list the *Apocalypse of Peter* as one of the "disputed books" 130 or more years later.

[8] This and all quotes from the Fragment here are taken from Bruce Metzger's translation: www.earlychristianwritings.com/text/muratorian -metzger.html.

Hermas the slave—we are still not sure what to make of that. Hippolytus himself, as we will see, later records the tale of Callistus, a runaway slave who became bishop of Rome in 218—so the very idea of a freedman in the chair of Peter was not, in itself, farfetched; but the *Muratorian Canon* is the only document that attempts to connect him with Hermas—and there are reasons to believe its author may not have intended the term to be taken literally. The main thing to gather at this point, however, is that the fragment's inclusion of *The Shepherd* shows Hippolytus (if he is, in fact, the author) and his commission (there are reasons to think the author did not work alone) trying to rule out a book that certainly did have the wide acceptance necessary on the grounds that it is not old enough, i.e., that it lacks apostolicity.

If it really is Hippolytus we are watching when we peek in at the Canonist working his problem, then he was only the first of several "A-list" names to tackle that job in the centuries to come. Origen, Cyril of Jerusalem, and Cyprian of Carthage all weighed in before the turn of the fourth century; and the makers of the four great uncial codices (regarded as the oldest existing copies of the Bible) all produced slightly different attempts at completing the same project.[9] If you were to examine all of these canons for

---

[9] All four contain—or once contained—practically all of the Septuagint, including its seven deuterocanonical books. Codex Vaticanus includes *Hebrews* but is missing the book of Revelation; Codex Sinaiticus includes Revelation but also contains *The Shepherd* and the Epistle of Barnabas; Codex Alexandrinus adds both 1st and 2nd Clement, along with 3rd and 4th Maccabees; while Codex Ephraemi is missing 2 Thessalonians and 2 John.

yourself, you might make an alarming discovery: that literally all of them—including our earliest copies of the Bible! —are deficient in some way by modern standards (whether our standards are Catholic, Protestant, or Eastern Orthodox). They all contain either too much or too little. They either leave out one or more of God's own inspired books, or they include man-made books that are not inspired at all. So the job going forward was one of reconciling all of these slightly different canons into one, universal Christian Bible for all the believers everywhere.

How did these scholars hope to resolve the puzzle? As we have seen, they looked: (1) for widespread liturgical use by churches known to have apostolic origins and (2) for actual signs of apostolicity—books, that is, that both claimed to be and were old enough to have credibly been written by or authorized by one of the twelve Apostles. What methods did Hippolytus and the others employ in their search? Alas, nobody knows! No record of their system has survived. Probably, the early canonists did their work by conferring with Christian librarians, archivists, and so forth, from the venerable churches that had always owned the books and had passed them down as "family heirlooms" through the decades. It is also likely that scholars like Hippolytus had access to other early records that are no longer available to us, these having perished or perhaps become lost like the Dead Sea Scrolls. The Muratorian Fragment, at any rate, preserves a snapshot of the work in progress as the job stood just prior to the turn of the third century at the venerable church of Rome.

The Apostolic Tradition

The younger Hippolytus wrote books of his own, of course —in fact, the old Catholic Encyclopedia calls him "the most prolific religious writer of the Roman Church in the pre-Constantinian era."[10] Most of these, however, exist only as fragments now; short quotations, many times, included in works by other writers. Even his most important work— *The Apostolic Tradition* of 215, which we previewed earlier— was attributed to other writers for many centuries and considered to be representative of the Eastern Church, not the Western, since all the surviving copies had been found in Egypt.[11] But once the scholarly legwork established Hippolytus as the real author, we finally realized what we had: "[The] *Apostolic Tradition* . . . is, with the exception of the *Didache*, the earliest and the most important of the ancient Christian Church Orders, . . . the richest source of information that we possess in any form for our knowledge of the constitution and life of the Church in the first three centuries."[12]

The title tells all, of course—chosen by Hippolytus himself. He is about to describe four of the great sacraments

---

[10] Article on "Hippolytus", in *CE*: www.newadvent.org/cathen/07360c .htm.

[11] "The title of the work is inscribed on the chair of the third-century statue of Hippolytus, but it was regarded as lost until E. Schwarz claimed in 1910, and R. H. Connolly demonstrated in 1916, that the Latin text of the so-called Egyptian Church Order represents substantially the Apostolic Tradition of Hippolytus. The Egyptian Church Order was so named merely because it became known to the modern world first in Ethiopic and Coptic translations": Johannes Quasten, *Patrology* (Allen, Tex.: Christian Classics, 1986), 2:181.

[12] Ibid., 2:180–81.

of the Church as we will come to know them in the ages ahead—and he wants us to know right off where his material comes from. This is a written description, he is insisting, of a set of rituals taught to the twelve Apostles (at least in embryonic form) by the Savior Himself and passed all the way down to the year A.D. 215 by their successors, the bishops in the apostolic succession. No, the instructions he will describe were not included within the pages of the New Testament—because they were already in place, already familiar to Christians as a workaday reality, before the New Testament books began to be written. As such, they represent a supreme example of that much-misunderstood term, *an unwritten tradition of the Church* that comes with the same authority as Scripture itself—because it has the very same source. And if Hippolytus really is the Canonist of Dr. Muratori's fragment, then he, himself, is a perfect illustration of how this process worked—for, in that case, we are watching one man participating in both processes! In the *Muratorian Canon*, Hippolytus worked to pass down the written tradition as it is contained in the genuinely apostolic books; and in *The Apostolic Tradition*, he strives to transmit the unwritten traditions he received from his predecessors contained in rituals dating back to the Upper Room itself.

The book begins with a description of *the rite of episcopal ordination*—the making of a new bishop, that is, through the laying on of hands. **"Let him be ordained bishop who has been chosen by all the people. When he has been appointed and approved by all, let the people come together with the college of [priests] and bishops who are present, on the Lord's Day. On the consent of all, let these latter lay their hands on him. The [priests] attend in silence. Let** all be quiet and pray in their hearts that the Holy Spirit may come down."[13]

Next follows the prayer of consecration—the "setting apart". "Let one of the bishops present, at the demand of all, lay his hands on him who is to receive episcopal ordination and pray in these terms."

> "God and Father of our Lord Jesus Christ, Father of mercy and all consolation, thou who dwellest in the highest of the heavens and dost lower thy regard to him who is humble,[14] who knowest all things before they exist; who hast fixed the bounds of thy Church by the word of thy grace; who hast predestined from the beginning the race of the just of Abraham; who hast established leaders and priests, who hast not left thy sanctuary without worship; who hast set thy pleasure, since the foundation of the world, in being glorified by those whom thou hast chosen: Pour out now the power which has its origin in thee, the sovereign Spirit whom thou hast given to thy beloved Child Jesus Christ and that he has handed on to the apostles who built the Church in place of thy sanctuary for the glory and unceasing praise of thy name."

The references to a Church built "in place of thy sanctuary", a sanctuary "not left without worship", indicate a belief that these rituals of New Testament worship have, by God's will, taken the place of the rites once performed by priests of the Old Covenant at the Jerusalem Temple. And

---

[13] All quotations from *The Apostolic Tradition* in this chapter are taken from *Early Sources of the Liturgy*, comp. and ed. Lucien Deiss, C.S.Sp. (New York: Alba House, 1967).

[14] The first phrase in this line is a citation of 2 Cor 1:3; the latter half is an allusion to Ps 113:5–6 as it appears in the Septuagint version.

as was the case under the Old Covenant, not just anyone is capable of carrying them out properly, but only those upon whom the power to do so has been poured out. Several of the earliest Fathers, in fact, go so far as to apply the word "Levites" to the recently minted line of New Covenant priests inaugurated by the Apostles. This is a clear indication that what we are witnessing here is the imparting of a real sacrament: soon to become known as the sacrament of Holy Orders.

"Grant, O Father", the rite continues, **"who readest the heart, that thy servant whom thou has chosen as bishop may feed thy holy flock, may exercise thy sovereign priesthood without reproach serving thee day and night. May he never cease to render thy regard favourable, and offer to thee the gifts of thy holy Church."** These gifts, as we will see in a moment, are the offerings of the Eucharistic table.

"In virtue of the Spirit of the supreme priesthood, may he have the power to forgive sins according to thy commandment.[15] May he . . . loose every bond in virtue of the power that thou hast conferred on the apostles." This power to loose bonds, which we briefly reviewed while considering Hermas and his Shepherd, is rooted in Christ's promise to the Apostles in Matthew 18:18: **"Truly, I say to you, whatever you bind on earth shall be bound in heaven, and whatever you loose on earth shall be loosed in heaven."**

May he [the new bishop] be pleasing to thee for gentleness and purity of heart. May he be before thee a sweet savour through thy Child Jesus Christ, our

---

[15] A reference to Jn 20:22–23.

Lord. Through him, glory to thee, power and honour, Father and Son, with the Holy Spirit, in thy holy
Church, now and always and for ever and ever! Amen.
      When he has been made a bishop, let all give him
the kiss of peace and acclaim him with the words: "He
has become worthy."

The ordination itself is now followed immediately by *a cel-
ebration of the Lord's Supper*—the first act of the new bishop's
episcopate.

"Let the deacons present the offering to him. When
he lays his hands on it, with the whole college of priests,
let him say the words of thanksgiving: 'The Lord be with
you.' " To this the people will answer: "And with thy spirit".
"Let us lift up our hearts", the bishop will continue, to be
answered with "They are turned to the Lord." "Let us
give thanks to the Lord"—"It is worthy and just."

"Eucharist", remember, means "the act of thanksgiving"
—and so the celebrant begins by giving thanks at length:

We give thee thanks, O God, through thy beloved
Child, Jesus Christ, whom thou hast sent to us in
the last times as Saviour, Redeemer and Messenger
of thy will. He is thine inseparable Word through
whom thou hast created all things and in whom thou
art well pleased.
      Thou didst send him from heaven into the womb of
a Virgin. He was conceived and became incarnate, he
manifested himself as thy Son, born of the Spirit and
the Virgin. He accomplished thy will and, to acquire a
holy people for thee, he stretched out his hands while
he suffered to deliver from suffering those who believe in thee.

In a kind of a footnote to this point, Hippolytus insists that "the bishop give thanks in the manner described above. It is not, however, necessary for him to use the form of words set out there, as though he had to make the effort to say them by heart in his thanksgiving to God." These opening prayers of thanksgiving, at least, need not be re-peated verbatim; in fact, Hippolytus, in his day, encourages the celebrant to ad-lib certain portions of the service. "Let each pray according to his abilities. If a man can make a becoming and worthy prayer, it is well. But if he prays in a different way, and yet with moderation, you must not prevent him, provided that the prayer is correct and con-forms to orthodoxy." Hippolytus himself, as a matter of fact, may have supplied us with material of his own in this very document; some of his wording at one or two points echoes Irenaeus' *Proof of the Apostolic Preaching*—so we may be looking there at recollected portions of the ritual which were originally composed by Hippolytus' old master.

Next up comes a solemn recollection of the institution of the sacrament, strongly echoing St. Paul's account in 1 Corinthians (11:23–25): "When he gave himself up will-ingly to suffering to destroy death, to break the fetters of the devil, to trample hell under his feet, to spread his light abroad over the just, to establish the Covenant and mani-fest his Resurrection, he took bread, he gave thee thanks and said: "Take, eat, this is my body which is broken for you." Likewise for the chalice, he said: 'This is my blood which is poured out for you. When you do this, do (it) in memory of me.'"

The kind of "remembering" our Lord called us to at

His Last Supper corresponds to the Hebrew term *zeker*—a special kind of remembrance that invites God, if you will allow it, to join the "nostalgia party" along with us. Employing our usual Greek, we Christians translate the word as *anamnesis*—a memory that calls down the thing remembered. The solemn remembrance to which Moses invited the Israelites—the Passover Seder—became, according to Jewish scholar Rabbi Yossi Kenigsberg, the only "Jewish holiday [where we are] instructed to have a formalized dialogue and discussion recollecting the relevant historical events of the time".[16] The text that sets forth the correct order of the Seder is known as the *Haggadah*, through which the memories of the Exodus are enacted in every Jewish home: **"Remember this day in which you came out from Egypt, out of the house of bondage, for by strength of hand the LORD brought you out from this place; no leavened bread shall be eaten. . . . You shall tell your son on that day, 'It is because of what the LORD did for me when I came out of Egypt.'. . . You shall therefore keep this ordinance at its appointed time from year to year"**—(Ex 13:3, 8, 10). The key phrase is "what the LORD did for me"—not just for previous generations; it is as though every Israelite has, himself, gone out of Egypt. Now, Hippolytus shows that we Christians are "not left without worship" of this type ourselves. In the New Covenant, the "exodus" was performed by Jesus on the Cross at Jerusalem;[17] and just

---

[16] Kenigsberg, "Observances and Rituals: The Seder, an Educational Experience", *The Jewish State*, April 25, 2008.

[17] Luke 9:31 tells us that Moses and Elijah "appeared in glory" to Jesus "and spoke of his exodus, which he was to accomplish at Jerusalem."

as under the Old Covenant, the act is meant to be ritually reenacted as an ordinance kept at its proper time; i.e., **"on the Lord's Day"**.

"We then," the liturgy continues, **"remembering thy death and thy Resurrection, offer thee bread and wine, we give thee thanks for having judged us worthy to stand before thee and serve thee. And we beg thee to send thy Holy Spirit upon the offering of thy holy Church, to gather and unite all those who receive it."** At this point, we recall the words of Paul once more: **"The cup of blessing which we bless, is it not a participation in the blood of Christ? The bread which we break, is it not a participation in the body of Christ? Because there is one bread, we who are many are one body, for we all partake of the one bread"** —(1 Cor 10:16–17).

"May they be filled with the Holy Spirit", prays the celebrant in conclusion, **"who strengthens their faith in the truth. So may we be able to praise and glorify thee through thy Child Jesus Christ. Through him, glory to thee, and honour, to the Father and to the Son, with the Holy Spirit, in thy holy Church, now and for ever. Amen."**

As the newly consecrated elements begin to be distributed to the faithful, the celebrant is invited to say: **"We entreat you again, almighty God, Father of our Lord Jesus Christ: grant us to receive this holy mystery with blessing."** Recalling the warnings, now, of St. Paul—that whoever **"eats the bread or drinks the cup of the Lord in an unworthy manner will be guilty of profaning the body and blood of the Lord"** and **"any one who eats and drinks without discerning the body, eats and drinks judgment upon**

himself"[18]—the new bishop prays: **"Do not condemn anyone among us. Let all those who receive this holy mystery be made worthy of the body and the blood of Christ,
almighty Lord, our God."**

"Then let [the faithful] **raise their hands to give glory.
Let the people draw near for the salvation of their souls.
Let them communicate that their sins may be forgiven
them."** This passage shows clearly that the Church already understood faith-filled reception of the Eucharistic
elements as one of the many powerful means our Lord established for the forgiving of post-baptismal sin.

Hippolytus provides public prayers for after Communion
as well: **"Almighty God, Father of the Lord and our Saviour
Jesus Christ, we give thee thanks for having granted us
to receive thy holy mystery. Let it not be a cause for us
of fault or of condemnation, but let it renew soul, body
and spirit, through thine only Son. Through him, glory to
thee and power, with him and the Holy Spirit, now and always and forever. Amen."** When they have communicated,

> **let the priest lay his hands on them and say: Everliv-
> ing, almighty God, Father of the Lord and our Saviour
> Jesus Christ, bless thy servants, men and women. Pro-
> tect them, uphold them, content them by the power of
> thine archangel. Guard them, strengthen in them awe
> in the presence of thy majesty. Give them peace with-
> out fear or anxiety, through thine only Son. Through
> him, glory to thee and power, with him and the Holy
> Spirit now and always and forever.**

---

[18] 1 Cor 11:27, 29.

Let the people reply: Amen. Let the bishop say: The Lord be with you. And let the people reply: And with thy spirit.

Finally, "**Let the deacon say: Go in peace. With that the sacrifice is finished.**"

More Apostolic Traditions

The second part of *The Apostolic Tradition* records the way that the early Church approached evangelism and the making of new Christians. That there were missionaries and other workers devoted chiefly to the spreading of the Gospel has already been established by our previous notices of Pantaenus and of Mark before him; and our earlier volume told the story of Irenaeus, not only a great theologian and bishop but a great foreign missionary. Something like what has come to be known as "life-style evangelism", however, must have been even more prominent; the danger of persecution was ever present, after all, and it had been Tertullian and his Montanists who denied believers the right to try and stay out of the way of harassing magistrates. Christians, at such times, surely emulated Christ's admonition to become "as wise as serpents" while still remaining "harmless as doves". History shows that even without explicit public testimony, many millions of pagans were drawn to the faith by the miraculous change they saw in their fellow Romans —and began to ask questions. Slowly, ever so carefully, their Christian friends must have begun to walk them through the answers.

"Those who are to be initiated into the new faith must first be brought to the catechists to hear the word, before the people arrive. They are to be asked their reasons for seeking the faith." Even before being allowed to attend church, in other words, the motives of inquirers were to be discerned. Some of the simplest rudiments of the faith were introduced and their reactions to them observed. **"Those who introduce them will bear witness in their regard in order that it may be known whether they are capable of hearing the Word."**

What was meant by "capable" here? Surely anyone who is not actually deaf is capable, is he not? Actually, this brings us back around to the preaching of Jesus Himself, who often spoke in obscure parables and then tested the reactions of His hearers: **"Let anyone with ears to hear listen!"** Both the Church and her Lord before her were, in using this principle, *looking for soil that the Father had already prepared in advance*. This is made clear by examining the Old Testament phrase that our Savior was referencing, Deuteronomy 29:4, where Moses used it to account for the widespread unbelief of the Israelites even after they had seen the great miracles of the Exodus: **"But to this day the LORD has not given you a mind to understand, or eyes to see, or ears to hear."** A teachable mind and a vulnerable heart are not only advantageous in prospective converts but absolutely indispensable, yet it is the Lord who sends them both.

What was the content of these earliest lessons? It can be deduced from the further instructions that were given to catechists: **"Their state of life also is to be scrutinized. . . . Enquiry is to be made about the trades and professions of those who are brought for instruction."** In this initial phase, then, evangelists were to lay all their cards on the table; inquirers were made aware that the call to Christianity begins with repentance and *always* includes life-style changes. As St. Paul told King Agrippa (Acts 26:19–20): **"I . . . declared first to those in Damascus, then in Jerusalem and throughout the countryside of Judea, and also to the Gentiles, that they should repent and turn to God and do deeds consistent with repentance."**

"If a man is a procurer," Hippolytus continues, **"that is to say, supports prostitutes, let him give it up or be sent away. . . . If he is a gladiator, or teaches gladiators to fight, or a hunter** [providing the wild animals to which Christians were often fed] **or if he is a public official who organises the gladiatorial games, let him give it up or be sent away. . . . If he is a priest of idols or a guardian of idols, let him give it up or be sent away. . . . Sorcerers, astrologers, fortune-tellers, interpreters of dreams, coiners** [possibly counterfeiters], **makers of amulets must give up these activities: otherwise they are to be sent away. . . . A man who has a concubine is to give her up and take a wife according to the law. If he refuses he is to be sent away."**

Notice that all of these renunciations are being asked of *still-heathen inquirers*—and not just asked, but verified by a period of probation: **"The catechumen is to attend the instruction for three years. However, if a man shows himself zealous and really perseveres in this undertaking, you are to judge him not by length of time but by his conduct."** Why on earth, one might wonder, are we judging a confessedly unbaptized sinner by his conduct? Is this an indication that the early Church believed redemption comes purely from "turning over a new leaf"—or that baptism might be

earned as a reward for clean living? By no means. As we
will see going forward, all of these requirements were really
meant to render the message of salvation *intelligible* when
the time came. All New Testament converts, for instance
—Cornelius, the Ethiopian eunuch, the Centurion at Ca-
pernaum—are remarkable for having readied themselves to
receive the Good News by means of a prior search and a
notable fear of God. St. John Henry Newman cites Proverbs
9:10 in this context: "The fear of the Lord is the beginning
of wisdom", and he does not forget, as so many do, to include the second clause; "all those who practice it have a
good understanding." This reflects the early Church's very
deep conviction that Truth can never really be found without sincere contrition and a genuine desire to live by God's
will once it is found.

Some have guessed that this long probationary period
was designed purely to weed out infiltrators, false converts
looking for reward money by uncovering nests of Christians. A fuller familiarity with the surviving records indicates that this was actually a minor consideration. The sea-
son of preparation laid out for converts was "enjoined", as
Newman continues, "in order to try their obedience". The
teaching they began to receive proceeded very slowly, "ad-
vancing from the most simple principle of Natural Religion
to the peculiar doctrines of the Gospel". According to Newman, the chief subjects of these earliest catechizings were,
"as we learn from Cyril [of Jerusalem], . . . the doctrines of
repentance and pardon, of the necessity of good works, of
the nature and use of baptism, and the immortality of the
soul".

Even after being formally accepted to the catechumenate, prospects were still given very little theology. "On their first admission they were denominated *hearers* [*euchomenoi*] from the leave granted them to attend the reading of the Scriptures and sermons in the Church"—but were escorted out of the service before the start of the common prayers. Writing of Clement, Cyril, Athanasius, and others, Newman noted that the early evangelists "would write, not with the openness of Christian familiarity, but with the tenderness or the reserve with which we are accustomed to address those . . . whom we fear to mislead or to prejudice against the truth, by precipitate disclosures of its details." The deeper truths of the faith, they believed, are not nourishing to unbelievers or catechumens; in fact, they can actually do more harm than good. Following St. Paul's lead in 1 Corinthians 2:14, the ancient catechists held that many doctrines can only be understood by minds previously illumined via the sacraments: **"The unspiritual man does not receive the gifts of the Spirit of God, for they are folly to him, and he is not able to understand them because they are spiritually discerned."**[19] This caution was, the Fathers believed, a "charitable consideration for those whom they addressed, who were likely to be perplexed, not converted, by the sudden exhibition of the whole evangelical scheme".

Late in the process, catechumens received a special laying on of hands similar to what we saw during the bishop's ordination; as a sign of their progress, they were now designated as *worshippers* and were, lastly, "taught the Lord's Prayer (the

---

[19] 1 Cor 2:14.

peculiar privilege of the regenerate), were entrusted with the knowledge of the [Apostles'] Creed, and, as destined for incorporation into the body of believers, received the titles of *competent* or *elect*"—capable, that is, of hearing. "Even to the last, they were granted nothing beyond a formal and general account of the articles of the Christian faith; the exact and fully developed doctrines of the Trinity and the Incarnation, and still more, the doctrine of the Atonement, as once made upon the cross, and commemorated and appropriated in the Eucharist, being the exclusive possession of the serious and practised Christian."[20]

"When", at the end of this lengthy process, **"those who are to be baptised have been chosen, their life is to be examined — whether they have lived devoutly during their catechumenate, whether they have respected widows, visited the sick, practised all the other good works. . . . If those who introduce them bear witness that they have been living in this way, let them hear the Gospel."**

The imparting of the sacrament itself was preceded by a vigil.

Those who are to be baptised must fast on the Friday and the Saturday. On the Saturday, the bishop gathers them all together in one place and bids them all pray and kneel. As he lays his hands on them, let him conjure all the foreign spirits to depart from them and never to return to them again. When he has finished the exorcism, let him breathe upon their faces, make the sign [of the cross] on their ears and nose

---

[20] John Henry Newman, *Arians of the Fourth Century* (London: Longmans Green, 1897), pp. 44–45, 47.

and then bid them rise and keep watch through the night.[21] They are to be given readings and instructions.

"At cockcrow, they are to come to the water; this must be running water and pure."[22] The elect then make a solemn renunciation of Satan and all his works, followed by a profession of faith as each article of the Creed is presented: "He who is baptising him lays his hand on his head and asks him: 'Dost thou believe in God, the almighty Father?' The one who is being baptised replies: 'I believe . . .' ", and so forth. "The children are baptised first. All those who can, are to reply for themselves. If they cannot, let their parents reply for them, or another member of the family."[23] All those being initiated are baptized three times—

---

[21] *The Apostolic Tradition* itself contains this valuable explanation for the Sign of the Cross, perhaps even the earliest account of its use: "At all times be ready to sign yourselves carefully on the forehead. For this sign shows forth the Passion which opposes the devil, if you make it with faith, not to please men, but knowing how to use it like a breastplate. Thus the adversary, seeing the power of the Spirit which comes from the heart, flies as soon as you show this spiritual likeness outwardly. . . . This is what Moses represented through the Passover lamb which was sacrificed, when he sprinkled the thresholds and smeared the doorposts with its blood. [The Fathers preserve a tradition that Moses made a 'cross-like' shape on the Israelite lintels]. It denoted the faith which we now have in the perfect Lamb. When we make the sign on our forehead and our eyes, we drive away him who seeks to destroy us."

[22] Hippolytus describes baptism under ideal circumstances. Necessity forced the Church to rule later on the validity of other methods and conditions, some of which were found valid while others were not.

[23] Early testimony to the acceptance of infant baptism in the Church; others can be found in the writings of Irenaeus, Tertullian, Origen, and Cyprian.

once for each of the Persons in the Triune formula. **"Then the priest gives him an anointing with the oil which has been sanctified. He says: 'I anoint thee with the oil which has been sanctified in the name of Jesus Christ.' After they have dried themselves, they put on their clothes again and go into the church."**

Perhaps surprisingly, the sacrament of confirmation was usually imparted immediately after baptism in those days.[24] **"As he lays his hands on** [the newly baptized], **the bishop invokes (God) saying: 'Lord God, who hast given to these the dignity of meriting the remission of their sins through the bath of regeneration of the Holy Spirit, fill them with thy grace that they may serve thee according to thy will. For to thee is the glory, Father and Son, with the Holy Spirit in the holy Church, now and for ever and ever. Amen."**

"Next, with his hand, he pours out the blessed oil.[25] He puts it on their heads saying . . . . 'The seal of the Holy Spirit.' " Hebrews 6:2 mentions both baptism and "the laying on of hands" in its list of "basic teaching about Christ" —and here, *The Apostolic Tradition* indicates that the "seal" imparted by this anointing with oil does, indeed, represent an even greater filling with the Spirit than baptism alone. As Jesus Himself was anointed "with the Holy Spirit and with power" (Acts 10:38) so we "little Christs" gain fuller power through the Church's sacrament of confirmation, "which in a certain way perpetuates the grace of Pentecost in the

---

[24] This is still the normal practice in the Eastern churches. Western Catholic bishops have been gradually lowering the age of confirmation in recent years.

[25] This oil, known as chrism, is still used in many of the rites of the ancient churches.

Church".²⁶ "**Next** [the priest] **marks them with the sign on the forehead, then he gives them a kiss saying: 'The Lord is with thee.' He who has been marked with the sign replies: 'And with thy spirit.' This is to be done for each of them.**"

"**From then on they are to pray with the whole people. But they are not to pray with the faithful until they have received all this. When they have prayed, let them give the kiss of peace.**" Finally, when all the sacraments of initiation have been given, "**each hastens to do good works, to please God and live a good life. He is to devote himself to the Church, putting what he has been taught into practice and making progress in the service of God.**"

The Two Popes

In 1851, we learned that Hippolytus, so careful and dispassionate as a scholar, was actually another hothead when away from his old manuscripts, one who eventually threw the same kind of grouchy fit as Tertullian. No, he did not join the Montanists, but he did stamp his feet about the very same issues that had caused Tertullian to lose his mind (over "the *Shepherd* of the Adulterers", etc.)—and during the same era. Uncovering this fact allowed scholars finally to reassemble all the chaotic notices of his life that had been dashed across time—the supposed stint as bishop of Rome, his alleged adherence to the schismatic Novatian, Eusebius'

---

²⁶ *Catechism of the Catholic Church*, 2d ed. (Rome: Libreria Editrice Vaticana; Washington, D.C.: United States Bishops' Conference, 2019), no. 1288.

inexplicable ignorance—into a story that finally made sense after more than 1700 years.

For many years, a third-century work called the *Philosophumena*, or *Refutation of All Heresies* (somewhat similar to Irenaeus' *Against Heresies*), was thought to have been written by Origen—even though, as the historian Theodoret pointed out way back in the fifth century, the Greek style in which it is written is not in the least similar to that of Origen. Initially divided into ten books, the *Philosophumena* as it existed until the nineteenth century was missing the entirety of books 2 and 3 and about the first half of book 4. These absent portions were finally discovered at Mt. Athos in 1842. Not long after that, someone realized that the newly uncovered titles lined up pretty well with the names on Pirro Ligorio's marble chair—and by the time they were edited and published nine years later, the biographical facts included in the new section had allowed experts to peg Hippolytus as the real author.

Biggest revelation of all, however? Our hero suddenly stood revealed as history's first antipope! In historical terms, an antipope is someone who made a significant attempt to occupy the Chair of Peter in opposition to the actual, duly elected bishop of Rome. Previously, the earliest of these was thought to have been Novatian himself, some twenty years after Hippolytus' death (more on this later). Hippolytus, in those once-missing books, is perfectly happy to disclose that he quarreled bitterly over theology with Pope Zephyrinus (who sat from 199 to 217) and came just short of rejecting his claim to the office.[27] But it was when Zephyrinus'

---

[27] In those years before the language of Trinitarian theology had been carefully worked out, churchmen often had trouble discussing the exact

deacon Callistus (yes, that ex-slave we mentioned earlier) succeeded him as pope that Hippolytus' wheels really came off. Not only did he accuse the new pope of holding the same alleged heresy as his predecessor, Hippolytus dug up and put an evil spin upon some unflattering facts from Callistus' past—he had apparently made, as a deacon, some bad investments with Church funds and thereby lost a lot of money belonging to Christian widows—and otherwise tried to blacken his name. Finally, when Callistus adopted the charitable attitude toward fallen-away sinners that, as we have already seen, drove Tertullian into schism, Hippolytus made his own decisive break with the Roman church. Taking a few disgruntled followers with him, he founded a rival congregation of his own at the capital and had himself declared the one and only true successor of St. Peter.

The fact that Hippolytus really was exaggerating the faults of Callistus is exposed by the jaundiced way in which he interprets all of his actions. **"The impostor Callistus"**, he

---

nature Christ's Divine Sonship without stumbling into verbal missteps that overemphasized one aspect of the subject or another. When seeking to underscore, for instance, that Christians still teach the ancient Monotheism of the Hebrews, theologians sometimes fell into the trap of *Modalism*, began talking, that is, as if Father and Son are just two different names for or manifestations of one single Divine Person. Reacting too violently against this, other interpreters slipped into something like *Ditheism*, making those two Divine Persons so distinct that it began to sound as if Christianity promotes the worship of two Gods, not One, whose unity is really only moral or symbolic. Hippolytus, at any rate, accused Zephyrinus of the former and appeared, in doing so, to slip over himself into the latter. The truth, probably, is that both men were simply limited human beings, trying to be orthodox, whose tongues got twisted when attempting to approach what really is the most profound mystery of our faith. Academic as they may seem, these distinctions later caused the great Arian crisis of the fourth century that almost swamped Christianity once and for all.

writes ("impostor" because Callistus still insisted on calling himself bishop of Rome) "... **established a school ... in antagonism to the Church**" ("the Church" meaning Hippolytus' new sect; the "school" meaning all those who stayed loyal to Callistus—the whole rest of Christendom, in other words!). Any foul adulterer or apostate who finds the door shut at the real (Hippolytan) church need only fly into the arms of the "impostor"; **"the sin, they say, is not reckoned unto him, provided only he hurries off** *and attaches himself* **to the school of Callistus."** Finally, Hippolytus makes one particularly illustrative charge: Callistus, he complains, even goes so far as to allow free women **"reputed [to be] believers"** to **"overturn their own dignity"** by choosing a slave **"as a bedfellow"** even though any such marriage was still illegal according to Roman civil law. This, at least, Pope Callistus really did do; he was the first Church leader to okay this minor deed of "civil disobedience" while acting in the spirit of St. Paul: **"there is neither slave nor free ... for you are all one in Christ Jesus"** (Gal 3:28). Even secular scholars agree that this was an important milestone on the centuries-long road to the abolition of slavery[28]—but Hippolytus, if you will, chose to respond after the familiar manner of Jim Crow. Surely, he predicts, the shame of

---

[28] Johannes Quasten, *Patrology* (Allen, Tex.: Christian Classics, 1986), 2:206–7. "The Roman Empire placed an insurmountable barrier between slave and free, stringently forbidding any marriage between them. Already prohibited by the Julian and Papian laws, such weddings were declared null and void by the Emperor Marcus and Commodus and reduced to the level of concubinage. . . . By giving her blessing in such cases, the Church broke down the barrier between the classes and treated their respective members as equals. . . ." Article "Callistus", in *CE*: "Here Callistus was rightly insisting on the distinction between the ecclesiastical law of marriage and the civil law, which later ages have always taught."

such unions will eventually drive these women to abortion or infanticide, **"on account of their not wishing to have a child either by a slave or by any paltry fellow, for the sake of their family"**. "Behold," he concludes, **"into how great impiety that lawless *one* has proceeded, by inculcating adultery and murder at the same time! And withal, after such audacious acts, they, lost to all shame, attempt to call themselves a Catholic Church!"[29]**

Plainly, strong feeling had overcome reason and faith once again. *The Apostolic Tradition* itself, so carefully preserved by none other than Hippolytus, included, recall, a recognition that bishops have just the power he was now denying: **"the power to forgive sins according to [Christ's] commandment"** and to **"loose every bond in virtue of the power . . . conferred on the apostles"**. And sadly, Hippolytus maintained his hostility to Callistus and his Church even after Callistus had been succeeded by Urban (in 222), and Urban by Pontian (in 230). Indeed, like a true curmudgeon, Hippolytus refused ever after to speak of that enormous Body as anything but "the school of Callistus" or its members by any name but Callistians.

All this changed, however, when yet another wave of persecution erupted in 235. The emperor Maximin Thrax (235–238), who seems to have hated Christians because his predecessor, Alexander, had been so friendly to them, ordered all Christian bishops put to death. His soldiers gathered up Hippolytans and Callistians with perfect indifference; and soon "the two popes", Hippolytus and Pontian, were banished and carried off together to the *Insula Novica* (the "Isle of Death")—perhaps on the same ship.

---

[29] Hippolytus, *Refutation of All Heresies*, bk. 9, chap. 7, *ANF* 5:131.

The forced labor facility on Sardinia—a lead mine sur-
rounded on all sides by fever swamps—actually was capital
punishment in slow motion; nothing but an extermination
camp, really, where inmates were quickly worked to death
if malaria did not take them first. Our bookish scholar, who
once labored to preserve apostolic traditions and to finalize
the canon of the New Testament, now dug ore out of the
earth with his bare hands and hauled it out of Stygian cav-
erns on his back. Ironically, Callistus himself had, as a young
man, been imprisoned for a while at the same camp—one of
the rare survivors. It may be, in other words, that Hippolytus found himself trying to sleep at night in a rat-infested
dungeon once occupied by the very man whose sympathy
for human weakness and regret had originally stirred him
to initiate his destructive schism. The name of Callistus, in
fact, might still have been visible, scratched onto the drip-
ping wall of his cell.

As their lives eked away, as the memory of church politics
and academic quarrels faded into irrelevance if not absurdity,
Pontian and Hippolytus became, once again, fellow Christians to one another—seeking solace from one another's
company. They must have tentatively, then wholeheartedly,
begun worshipping together, praying together—and then
praying together for the flock back home. "Communion
in suffering", as the Spiritan priest Lucien Deiss wrote,
"opened the way to communion in faith and charity."[30]
The "two popes" decided, at any rate, to do something
magnificent for those they had left behind. On September
28, 235, Pontian resigned his office (the first pope ever to

---

[30] Deiss, *Early Sources of the Liturgy*, p. 31.

do so) and Hippolytus renounced his own claims to the same chair, sending the news back to Rome, clearing the way for the election of a single new bishop and freeing all of their followers to put the schism behind them. The new and undoubted pope, Anterus, was chosen on the 21st day of November in the same year.

Anterus, sadly, was caught up in the same persecution himself; he presided over the Roman church only forty days. He may actually have predeceased Pontian and Hippolytus, but not, surely, by much. Both of them were certainly dead by the summer of 236, for Pope Fabian (236–250) arranged for their bodies to be brought back from Sardinia to Rome, where a joint funeral was held on August 13. Pontian is still buried in the papal vault in the catacombs named for Callistus; Hippolytus rests in the cemetery that carries his own name, located along the Via Tiburtina. Soon both saints were being equally revered as martyrs at Rome, "certain proof that Hippolytus had made his peace with that Church before his death".[31]

This is how Hippolytus, schismatic and antipope, a mere Roman presbyter who claimed to be bishop and was nevertheless venerated as hero and martyr and had a statue made and a hymn written in his honor, could be mentioned as a Novatianist (a slight chronological mistake)[32] by a real pope decorating his grave. This is why his name is missing from the Liberian Catalogue; this is why the *Philosophumena* was

---

[31] Article "Hippolytus", in *CE*.

[32] Novatian did not begin his career as a heretic until twenty-five or more years after the death of Hippolytus. His did, however, become the name most associated with the rigorist heresy—even though Tertullian and Hippolytus both anticipated the error.

deliberately preserved without books 2 and 3 or the first half of book 4—minus, that is, the nasty screed against Callistus. We ourselves might almost wish, as his friends undoubtedly wished, that those portions had never been found—were it not for the fact that we should, in that case, never have known this beautiful story of the grace and mercy of Christ, friend of sinners.

Origen Adamantius

His father, Leonides, knew there was something special about him early on. **"They say that often, standing by the boy when asleep, he uncovered his breast as if the Divine Spirit were enshrined within it, and kissed it reverently"**, considering himself blessed to have been entrusted with the care of a child so hungry for God. He tried to satisfy that hunger with knowledge; not only, as a Christian father, with knowledge of the Bible, but with the rudiments of science, mathematics, and literature as well. The Scriptures were his son's special delight, however, and Leonides **"drilled him in sacred studies, requiring him to learn and recite every day. Nor was this irksome to the boy, but he was eager and diligent in these studies."** The lad benefitted in this by a knowledge of Hebrew, a rare ability in a Christian scholar in those days, which he may have picked up in the home from a mother of Jewish descent.[1] **"And he was not satisfied with learning what was simple and obvious in the sacred words, but sought for something more, and even at that age busied himself with deeper speculations"**—so much so that he often stumped his father with profound or difficult questions. Leonides sometimes scolded him for this, warning him about getting in over his head, about wandering away from the tried and true path; but secretly,

---

[1] Porphyry, at any rate, tells us that Origen could sing the Psalms in their original language and did it so well that "he vied with his mother."

"he rejoiced greatly and thanked God, the author of all good,"[2] for the privilege of watching such a mind at work. Oldest of his six children, the boy had been given by his father the Greek name *Origenes*, which we English-speakers traditionally convert to Origen.

When Origen was still just a teenager, the bloody persecution of Septimius Severus broke out in Roman Egypt. Before long, his father was caught up in it, carried away to a dungeon, threatened with beheading if he would not earn his release by renouncing Christ and sacrificing to the gods. Origen became frantic to join him, to win a martyr's crown at his father's side. His mother, equally frantic to save her son's life, only prevented him from doing so by hiding his clothes!—so that he could not turn himself in to the magistrate without looking like a madman and thereby discrediting his faith. Frustrated, he settled for writing an anguished but deeply heartfelt letter to his father in prison. Origen knew just as well as Leonides that all of his family's property would be forfeit to the imperial treasury if his father did not submit; his wife and children would be turned out into the street. He also knew that Christian men before Leonides had wavered with just this thought in mind. Origen wrote, then, with a **"zeal beyond his age"**, exhorting his father to stand fast and not to yield for his sake or for any worldly consideration: **"Take heed not to change your mind on our account."** "This", as Eusebius concludes, **"may be recorded as the first evidence of Origen's youthful wisdom and of his genuine love**

---

[2] Eusebius, *Church History*, bk. 6, chap. 2: www.newadvent.org/fathers/250106.htm.

for piety." Leonides went to the block right on schedule.

Origen did finally succeed in joining his father in martyrdom—but only some fifty years later. In between came a life so brilliant, so exemplary, so downright holy that some have considered him perhaps the greatest of all the ante-Nicene Fathers. In simplicity and asceticism, he was a third-century Francis of Assisi; in his familiarity with and understanding of the holy Scriptures, he was at least the equal of his contemporary, Jerome. The vast intellect his father had detected made him a genuine prodigy; he succeeded Clement of Alexandria as headmaster at the Catechetical School at the ripe old age of eighteen. He used that position to become one of the foremost evangelists of his time: **"Origen's school, which was frequented by pagans, soon became a nursery of neophytes, confessors, and martyrs."**[3] Eventually, Julia Mamaea, the mother of a future Emperor, heard of Origen's fame and invited him to Antioch to hear his teaching. Her son Alexander (who ruled the empire from 222 to 235) likely heard as well; since, according to his biographer Lampridius, he later placed a bust of Jesus in his private chapel (along with images of the pagan sages Orpheus and Apollonius of Tyana) and caused our Lord's words from Luke's Gospel to be engraved on the walls of the palace of the Caesars: "As ye would that men should do to you, do ye also to them likewise."[4] **"They say"**, as Eusebius wrote

---

[3] Article "Origen and Origenism", in *CE*: www.newadvent.org/fathers/11306b.htm.

[4] Claims, nevertheless, that Alexander Severus was actually the first Christian emperor—some eighty years before Constantine—are overstated. At best, he seems to have been, like King Agrippa in Acts 26, "almost persuaded to be a Christian".

in his eulogy, **"that [Origen's] manner of life was as his doctrine, and his doctrine as his life. Therefore, by the divine Power working with him he aroused a great many to his own zeal."**[5]

All this being the case, how comes it to pass that the name of Origen *is not* invoked at our altars? Even Hippolytus, after all, achieved that honor despite all his many faults. Why have the great ancient churches not recognized Origen officially as a saint? The answer is, well, complicated. But it is also very, very instructive as a way to illustrate what the Fathers *are* and *are not* good for in today's Christianity . . . which will be the theme of this final chapter.

Man of Steel

When Origen became man of the house just short of his eighteenth birthday and found himself acting as sole support for a mother and five younger siblings, he did not turn, as many of us would have, to the cutting of grass or the shoveling of snow (a good thing, too, since it never snows in Alexandria). Origen already had, after all, several years it seems of excellent (if illegal) schooling under his belt. His teacher?—Clement himself, at the Catechetical School. Closed now on account of the persecution, the school had been unwillingly abandoned when Clement, with a price on his head, fled into exile. Thus, Origen was free to liquidate, though most reluctantly, his old schoolbooks, many of which were valuable philosophical and poetical works by pagan authors—and thus quite saleable for quick cash.

---

[5] Eusebius, *Church History*, bk. 6, chap. 2.

When this money ran out, he put his own liberal education to work, tutoring pagan students in grammar and science from a small, private schoolhouse. His God-given gifts along these lines became so obvious that his local pastor picked Origen to teach the faith to catechumens preparing for baptism, a job usually reserved for a much older man. Finally, after so many of his own former classmates gravitated in the same direction, Origen found himself doing Clement's old job by default. Demetrius, bishop of Alexandria at the time, found out about this . . . and made it official within a year. A teenager sat in the seat of Pantaenus.

Like the boys who went into the trenches during the Great War, Origen the teenager grew up quickly. In fact, he really was a "wartime" headmaster, since his students constantly failed to show up for class, having fallen into the hands of the authorities overnight. Since such captives were routinely put to torture in an effort to uncover the names of their co-religionists, the danger of a raid on Origen's classes was perpetual. So many Christians were frightened away from the school, in fact, that **"some of the heathen came to him to hear the word of God"** in their places, drawn by the heroism and conviction of the teacher. **"He restrained himself as much as possible by a most philosophic life; sometimes by the discipline of fasting, again by limited time for sleep. And in his zeal he never lay upon a bed, but upon the ground. . . . Most of all, he thought that the words of the Saviour in the Gospel should be observed, in which he exhorts not to have two coats nor to use shoes nor to occupy oneself with cares for the future."** Those who imagine some kind of inherent disconnect between "head knowledge" and "heart knowledge" have not met men like

Origen. "By giving such evidences of a philosophic life to those who saw him, he aroused many of his pupils to similar zeal; so that prominent men even of the unbelieving heathen and men that followed learning and philosophy were led to his instruction. Some of them having received from him into the depth of their souls faith in the Divine Word, became prominent in the persecution then prevailing; and some of them were seized and suffered martyrdom." Among these Eusebius lists by name, Plutarch,[6] Serenus, Heraclides, Hero, another Serenus, and a female catechumen, Herais, all of whom, "after living well, [were] honored with divine martyrdom."

And when they were "led to death, [Origen] was very bold and went with them into danger. . . . [H]e acted bravely, and with great boldness saluted the martyrs with a kiss, [and] oftentimes the heathen multitude round about them became infuriated, and were on the point of rushing upon him. But through the helping hand of God, he escaped absolutely and marvelously." God Himself intervened, Eusebius believed, to keep Origen's school open.

> This same divine and heavenly power, again and again, it is impossible to say how often, on account of his great zeal and boldness for the words of Christ, guarded him when thus endangered. So great was the enmity of the unbelievers toward him, on account of the multitude that were instructed by him in the sacred faith, that they placed bands of soldiers around the house where he abode. Thus day by day the persecution burned against him, so that the whole city could no longer

---

[6] Not to be confused with the first-century historian or the fourth-century Neoplatonist philosopher.

contain him; but he removed from house to house and was driven in every direction because of the multitude who attended upon the divine instruction which he gave. For his life also exhibited right and admirable conduct according to the practice of genuine philosophy.[7]

It was probably during this period that he was given his traditional honorific of Adamantius, the Man of Steel.

It may also have been at this time that Origen, feeling the pressure of his unaccustomed status as a role model, committed the biggest blunder of his career. In an act that may have been more shocking to earlier Christian readers, less experienced than we are with the terrible toll of guilt on young people, of the near impossibility of true purity brought about by growing up in a sex-saturated pagan culture, where even great Church leaders are continually brought low by a public fall into immorality, Origen took our Lord's words in Matthew 19:12 much too literally: **"there are eunuchs who have made themselves eunuchs for the sake of the kingdom of heaven."** He had himself castrated—an act that was against Church law even at the time. **"To take away from the unbelievers all opportunity for scandal—for, although young, he met for the study of divine things with women as well as men—he carried out in action the word of the Saviour."** He must have done it in a moment of anguish, for he seems to have regretted the deed immediately, hoping that it would not become known to any of his acquaintances. **"But it was impossible for him, though desiring to do so, to keep such an action secret."**

---

[7] Eusebius, *Church History*, bk. 6, chap. 3.

Later, when he had acquired enemies within the Church as well as without, this act **"which evidenced an immature and youthful mind"**[8] was constantly thrown into his teeth.

Needless to say, Origen, in his teaching, followed "the Alexandrian Method" he had learned under Clement. In fact, he continued his avid study of pagan philosophy even as a Christian catechist hounded by pagans. **"Nor is it appropriate, because we hold a law to be given by God, for us to swell with pride and despise the words of the prudent"**, he once explained. **"But, as the Apostle says, we should 'prove all things and hold fast that which is good.'"**[9] He personally attended lectures by Ammonius Saccas, mentor of the great Plotinus. He continued his own careful studies of Plato, Aristotle, and Zeno. And whenever he perceived that any of his Christian students **"had superior intelligence he instructed them also in philosophic branches—in geometry, arithmetic, and other preparatory studies—and then advanced to the systems of the philosophers and explained their writings . . . saying that these would be no small help to them in the study and understanding of the Divine Scriptures."**[10] He also prefigured the later work of St. Jerome in honing his Hebrew skills by placing himself under the tutelage of learned rabbinical Jews. This does not mean, of course, that he neglected his Christian stud-

---

[8] Ibid., chap. 8.

[9] Origen, Homily XI on Exodus, in *Homilies on Genesis and Exodus*, trans. Ronald E. Heine, Fathers of the Church, vol. 71 (Washington, D.C.: Catholic Univ. of America Press, 1982) p. 364. See 1 Thess 5:21 and also Greg. Thaumaturgis, *Oration and Panegyric Addressed to Origen*, chap. 15: www.newadvent.org/fathers/0604.htm.

[10] Eusebius, *Church History*, bk. 6, chap. 18.

ies in the slightest. While still in his twenties, for instance, Origen made a special trip to Italy **"when Zephyrinus was bishop of Rome . . . 'desiring,' as he himself somewhere says, 'to see the most ancient church of Rome.'"**[11] He attended services there and heard Hippolytus himself, still a priest in good standing, preach a homily "On the Praise of the Lord Our Savior".

Origen used typically Alexandrian allegorism in his theology, too—more freely even than Clement had. Unlike rival interpreter Marcion, whose heresy pitting an "Old Testament God of wrath" against a "New Testament God of love" was still going strong at the time, Origen believed the two covenants of Scripture *could* be harmonized, but only by using allegory to uncover the spiritual meaning of the Hebrew writings hidden under the grotesqueries and archaisms. As precedent for this, he could point to St. Paul, who saw the relationship between the Church and the Synagogue prefigured in the strange, primordial story of Isaac and Ishmael: **"Now this is an allegory: these women are two covenants. One is from Mount Sinai, bearing children for slavery; she is Hagar . . . [but] we, brethren, like Isaac, are children of promise."**[12] Perhaps ironically, given what we have just learned about his approach to "those who made themselves eunuchs", Origen believed most errors of interpretation came about when readers took Bible passages too literally—or, perhaps better, took them too exclusively in the literal sense (as, for instance, when Marcion used Exodus 32:14—**"And the LORD repented of the**

---

[11] Ibid., chap. 14.
[12] The full allegory is found in Gal 4:21–31.

evil which he thought to do to his people"—to prove that
the Old Testament God could not possibly be the father of
Christ, **"with whom there is no variation or shadow due to
change"**—Jas 1:17). Any given portion of Scripture may be
interpreted in several distinct, complementary senses, he believed—without necessarily creating contradictions. Grasp
the literal meaning first, Origen taught, then compare it
with other passages to gain additional light.

Readers who may have foreseen danger in this approach,
whether here or while we were discussing St. Clement, are
not wrong. However defensible in the abstract, there really
is some inherent risk in "going outside the cloister" in the
Alexandrian way, seeking input from secular teachers, that
is, or adherents of some other religion. And Origen's allegorical flights can, indeed, seem arbitrary at times, skirting
the boundaries of *eisegesis*—the reading of one's own opinions *into* a given scriptural text rather than extracting God's
meaning out. His elucidation of the parable of the Good
Samaritan, for instance, is renowned:

> The man who was going down is Adam. Jerusalem is
> paradise, and Jericho is the world. The robbers are
> hostile powers. The priest is the law, the Levite is the
> prophets, and the Samaritan is Christ. The wounds
> are disobedience. The beast is the Lord's body. The
> *pandochium* (that is, the stable), which accepts all who
> wish to enter, is the church. The two denarii mean
> the Father and the Son. The manager of the stable
> is the head of the church, to whom its care has been
> entrusted. The fact that the Samaritan promises he
> will return represents the Savior's second coming.[13]

---

[13] *Homilies on the Gospel of Luke* 34.3, 9.22. Quoted in *Ancient Christian Commentary on Scripture: New Testament*, vol. 3, ed. Arthur Just, Jr.

The famous modernist theologian Adolf Harnack, especially hostile to Greek influence on early Christianity, called this "biblical alchemy".

The Man of Steel charged right ahead, nonetheless. How is it that he felt so safe? Simply put, Origen was the disciple of Clement of Alexandria. Clement had taught "the Alexandrian method", of course, but he is also the one who taught us that **"maintaining apostolic and ecclesiastic orthodoxy in doctrines"**[14] provides the guardrails, a safety net that makes "going out on a limb" after the manner of Origen not only a legitimate but even a praiseworthy occupation. Bible readers *ought* to share their own unique reactions to Scripture; and, like Hermas' dreams, these personal interactions with the Holy Spirit can be shared with everyone, because they are not *binding* on anyone. All that is necessary to secure this kind of freedom is the willingness always to give the apostolic Church, speaking through her authorized ministers, the final say. And this attitude of humility was always apparent in everything that Origen did; indeed, he called himself **"a man of the Church"** first and foremost. **"We should not listen to those who say, 'Look! Here is Christ!' — but do not point him out in the Church, which is full of his radiance from east to west, which is full of true light, which is the pillar and foundation of**

(Downer's Grove, Ill.: InterVarsity Press, 2003), p. 180.—However subjective it may strike us nowadays, Origen's language here parallels that of our Lord exactly as He elucidated another of His parables: "Parable of the Sower" (Mt 13:1–23). If allegory has been used in the Bible itself as an instrument of communication of biblical truth, then using allegory for the purpose of preaching cannot possibly be considered simply wrong.

[14] Clement, *Stromata*, bk. 7, chap. 16: www.newadvent.org/fathers/02107 .htm.

truth."[15] This was a hard and fast rule for him and an example for us: "**[T]hat alone is to be accepted as truth which
differs in no respect from ecclesiastical and apostolic tradition.**"[16] And Origen stuck with this to the end.

The God-Bearer

Perhaps surprisingly for a system based in tradition, theology was not seen as a static science for the early Christians;
the Holy Spirit has not stopped teaching the Church merely
because new public revelation is no longer to be expected.
Yes, as Irenaeus wrote, "**the apostles, like a rich man**" making a deposit in a bank, "**lodged in her hands most copi-
ously all things pertaining to the truth.**"[17] Nevertheless,
"**every scribe who has been trained for the kingdom of
heaven**", Jesus taught, "**is like a householder who brings
out of his treasure what is new and what is old.**"[18] Apostolic tradition acts as a solid foundation, but that foundation, just as in a construction project, was always intended
to support an ever-rising edifice, like the tower in Hermas'
vision of the Church. By the judicious application of imagination and insight (qualities a man like Origen possessed in
great abundance), the Church's thinkers may interpret and
more thoroughly digest that original deposit in such a way as
to make possible continual withdrawals from the apostolic
bank, to the enrichment of every believer. The Advocate,

---

[15] Origen, *Commentary on St. John's Gospel*, 6: in Mike Aquilina, *Villains
of the Early Church* (Steubenville, Ohio: Emmaus Road, 2018), 104. "Pillar
and foundation" is a reference to 1 Tim 3:15.

[16] Origen, *De Principiis*, Preface, *ANF*: newadvent.org/fathers/04120.htm.

[17] Irenaeus, *Against Heresies*, bk. 3, chap. 4, *ANF*: www.newadvent.org/
fathers/0103304.htm.

[18] Mt 13:51.

as our Savior said, **"the Holy Spirit, whom the Father will send in my name, he will teach you all things, and bring to your remembrance all that I have said to you."**[19]

As a way to illustrate this ongoing process, it might be helpful to review briefly the manner in which God gradually unveiled the outlines of the greatest mystery of them all: the dogma of the Blessed Trinity. As most believers realize, the word "Trinity" itself does not appear in Scripture, nor do any of the later formulations we associate with it: "the Triune Godhead", "God in three Persons", and so forth. The *raw material* for those terms is in the Bible, of course, but still "packed up", so to speak, rather like ore in a mineral deposit, waiting to be excavated and hammered into something more immediately useful. The actual word only starts to appear once the Fathers have begun their work—first, *Trias* in Greek, in a letter of Theophilus written about 180, then *Trinitas* in Latin, in Tertullian's *On Modesty*, about 220[20]—but even then, it is not used in exactly the right sense for many years to come. Most, if not all, of the ante-Nicene Fathers, in fact—including Justin, Irenaeus, Hippolytus, and, yes, Origen—fumbled their way into various faulty Trinitarian analogies sooner or later, as many of us laypersons have found ourselves doing since then. Yes, those statements are defective by the standards of the later Nicene and Athanasian Creeds; and yes, those statements would have to be ruled heretical if offered today. But the fourth- and fifth-century creed-makers were only able to do their work *because* of these mistakes; the false starts endured by these earlier lights, and their many almost-right

---

[19] Jn 14:26.
[20] Ironically, *On Modesty* is one of Tertullian's Montanist works.

solutions, provided the data that the whole Church finally sifted and collated to reach the correct answer. St. Gregory of Nazianzus, one of the major figures involved in the sifting, looked back on the process this way:

> **The Old Testament proclaimed the Father openly, and the Son more obscurely. The New manifested the Son, and suggested the Deity of the Spirit. Now the Spirit Himself dwells among us, and supplies us with a clearer demonstration of Himself. For it was not safe, when the Godhead of the Father was not yet acknowledged, plainly to proclaim the Son; nor when that of the Son was not yet received to burden us further (if I may use so bold an expression) with the Holy Ghost; lest perhaps people might, like men loaded with food beyond their strength, and presenting eyes as yet too weak to bear it to the sun's light, risk the loss even of that which was within the reach of their powers.**

The complete truth, St. Gregory concludes, was unpacked **"by gradual additions . . . [by] advances and progress from glory to glory"**, so that finally, **"the Light of the Trinity might shine upon the more illuminated."**[21]

Something like this happened with another important topic as well, the early Church's devotion to the Mother of Christ—and there, Origen played a major role. The John Rylands University Library in Manchester, England, owns a piece of papyrus found in Egypt dating from about the year 250—right around the time of Origen's death. On it are the words of an ancient petition addressed to the Vir-

---

[21] Gregory Nazianzen, *Fifth Theological Oration*, chap. 26: www.newadvent.org/fathers/310231.htm.

gin Mary, possibly used in church services: **"Under your mercy we take refuge, O Mother of God. Do not reject our supplications in necessity, but deliver us from danger, only pure, only blessed one."** The Greek word translated as "Mother of God" is *Theotokos*, more literally rendered as "God-bearer"—the one who bore God in her womb and gave Him birth as a Man into the world of men. Like "Trinity", this word *Theotokos* is not found in Scripture, though the building materials were present all along, waiting to be unpacked. We see here that the term was finished for use by 250, so like *Trinitas* it must have had a long gestation period in the years beforehand. And the workmen, as in that other job, were the early Church Fathers.[22]

Though it sounds very alien to Evangelical ears, the term "Mother of God" is really more about Jesus than Mary: **"that holy thing which shall be born of thee shall be called the Son of God"** (Lk 1:35).[23] *Theotokos* arose, as a matter of fact, under pressure from the Docetists: those heretical enemies of Ignatius Theophorus, who denied that God the Son had really come in the flesh. In their gnostic system, a Divine Being had appeared on earth *as if He were a man*, a bit of heavenly role-playing undertaken purely as a way to interface more readily with mortals. St. Ignatius, the Church's first great champion against this error, highlighted Mary's role early on (about A.D. 107) in a collection of biblical proofs to the contrary: **"[The Lord] was truly of the**

---

[22] "As it is admitted that the praises of Mary grow with the growth of the Christian community, we may conclude in brief that the veneration of and devotion to Mary began even in the time of the Apostles": article "Virtue", in *CE*.

[23] KJV.

seed of David according to the flesh, . . . and the Son of
God according to the will and power of God; that He was
truly born of a virgin, was baptized by John, in order that
all righteousness might be fulfilled . . . by Him; and was
truly, under Pontius Pilate and Herod the tetrarch, nailed
[to the cross] for us in His flesh."[24] God is truly incarnate
in the man Christ Jesus; and Mary is truly the mother of
that Man.[25]

St. Justin Martyr, a few decades later, can be seen ponder-
ing the mystery more deeply; reading the story of Mary in
light of St. Paul's great insight depicting Jesus as a "Second
Adam": **"For as by a man came death,"** wrote the Apostle,[26] **"by a man has come also the resurrection of the dead.
For as in Adam all die, so also in Christ shall all be made**

---

[24] Ignatius, *To the Smyrnaeans*, chap. 1: www.newadvent.org/fathers/0109
.htm.

[25] The great apologist Cardinal Gibbons clarified some of the issues involved: "It may be [objected that] the Blessed Virgin is not the Mother
of the Divinity. 'She had not, and she could not have, any part in the generation of the Word of God, for that generation is eternal; her maternity
is temporal. He is her Creator; she is His creature. Style her, if you will,
the Mother of the man Jesus or even of the human nature of the Son of
God, but not the Mother of God.' I shall answer this objection by putting
a question. Did the mother who bore us have any part in the production
of our *soul*? Was not this nobler part of our being the work of God alone?
And yet who would for a moment dream of saying 'the mother of my body,'
and not '*my* mother?' . . . In like manner, . . . the Blessed Virgin, under
the overshadowing of the Holy Ghost, by communicating to the Second
Person of the Adorable Trinity, as mothers do, a true human nature of the
same substance with her own, is thereby really and truly His Mother . . .
in this sense, and in no other, has the Church called her by that title": *The
Faith of Our Fathers*, rev. ed. (New York: P. J. Kenedy & Sons, 1917), pp.
137–38.

[26] 1 Cor 15:21–22.

ORIGEN ADAMANTIUS   149

alive." Justin, in his *Dialogue with Trypho*, takes up this profound Garden of Eden parallel, realizing that in it, Mary
the Virgin acts the part of the new Eve:

> **[The Son of God] became man by the Virgin, in order
> that the disobedience which proceeded from the ser-
> pent might receive its destruction in the same man-
> ner in which it derived its origin. For Eve, who was
> a virgin and undefiled, having conceived the word of
> the serpent, brought forth disobedience and death.
> But the Virgin Mary received faith and joy, when the
> angel Gabriel announced the good tidings to her that
> the Spirit of the Lord would come upon her, and the
> power of the Highest would overshadow her: where-
> fore also the Holy Thing begotten of her is the Son
> of God; and she replied, "Be it unto me according to
> your word."[27] And by her has He been born, to whom
> we have proved so many Scriptures refer, and by whom
> God destroys both the serpent and those angels and
> men who are like him.[28]**

St. Irenaeus of Lyons, not long afterward, took up Justin's
intuition and expanded upon it: **"Adam had necessarily to
be restored in Christ, that mortality be absorbed in immortality, and Eve in Mary, that a virgin, become the advocate of a virgin, should undo and destroy virginal disobedience by virginal obedience."[29]**

God's plan of salvation, to put the matter shortly, was
"Adam and Eve in reverse". As patristic scholar Luigi

---

[27] Lk 1:38.

[28] Justin Martyr, *Dialogue with Trypho*, chap. 100: www.newadvent.org/fat
hers/01287.htm.

[29] Irenaeus, *Proof of the Apostolic Preaching*, chap. 33, ACW, vol. 16 (New
York: Paulist Press, 1952), p. 69.

Gambero puts it, "Mary has a role in relation to Christ, the second Adam, just as the first Eve had a role in relation to the first Adam."[30] **"By disobeying,"** Irenaeus continues, **"Eve became the cause of death for herself and for the whole human race. In the same way Mary, though she also had a husband, was still a virgin, and by obeying, she became the cause of salvation for herself and for the whole human race."[31]** As Eve had her part in the Fall of humanity (though the final work was accomplished by Adam), so did Mary take a role in humanity's redemption—not as the actual redeemer, mind you, but as one who, by her obedience, played an indispensable part in setting the stage for His unique work.

Irenaeus also perceived that a mature understanding of Mary's role acts as a powerful antidote to the Docetist mix-up: **"The apostle Paul, in his letter to the Galatians, clearly states that 'God sent his Son, born of a woman'"** (Gal 4:4). **And in his letter to the Romans, he says, 'His son, born of David's seed according to the flesh, constituted Son of God in power, according to the Spirit of holiness that raised him from the dead, Jesus Christ our Lord.'** (Rom 1:3–4). **Had it been otherwise, his descent into Mary would have been superfluous."[32]** Mary, in other words, is our necessary guarantee of the humanity of Christ. Already there were those who—staggering, perhaps, at the profundity of the doctrine of the Incarnation—wished to see Mary as a mere conduit for God's messenger, providing nothing her-

---

[30] Luigi Gambero, *Mary and the Fathers of the Church* (San Francisco: Ignatius Press, 1999), p. 46.

[31] Irenaeus, *Adversus haereses* 3:22, quoted in ibid., p. 58.

[32] Ibid., p. 57.

self, acting more like a surrogate mother than a real one. To this Irenaeus responds with a question:

> For why would he have descended within her, if he did not need to take something from her? Furthermore, if he had not taken anything from Mary, [Jesus] would not have been accustomed to eating earthly food . . . nor, after fasting forty days, like Moses and Elijah, would he have felt hunger pangs (cf. Mt 4:2), and if his body had not felt the need for nourishment, neither would his disciple John have written of him: "Jesus, tired from the journey, sat down" (Jn 4:6). . . . Nor would he have wept over Lazarus (cf. Jn 11:35) or sweated drops of blood (Mt 26:38) or said, "My soul is exceedingly sad" (cf. Jn 19:34), nor would blood and water have flowed from his pierced side (cf. Jn 19:34). These are all signs that he took flesh from the earth, recapitulating this flesh in himself to save his own creation. . . . In accordance with this design, the Virgin Mary was found obedient when she said, "Behold your handmaid, O Lord; let it be done to me according to your word" (Lk 1:38).[33]

In all this, Irenaeus was simply echoing once again Ignatius of Antioch, disciple of St. John the Apostle, in his own battles against Docetism: "There is one Physician, who is both flesh and spirit, born and not born, who is God in man, true life in death, both from Mary and from God, first able to suffer and then unable to suffer, Jesus Christ our Lord."[34]

Yet just as in the matter of the Trinity, there were staggerers even among the Fathers; early lights who, in spite

---

[33] Ibid., pp. 57–58.
[34] *FEF* 1:18, no. 39.

of their wisdom, made unfortunate blunders. Tertullian, for instance, sets himself against several aspects of the traditional doctrine; and even Clement of Alexandria, Origen's own tutor, allowed his allegorism to lead him into dicey conclusions about Mary—as, for instance, when he maintained that our Lord's mother did not nurse her Son in the normal way because Christ is spiritual and the Word of God was his "milk", His only necessary nourishment.

Here is where Origen came to the rescue. Stepping in to clarify his master's missteps, Origen reemphasized the essential truth that Mary's motherhood is real and factual, part of the natural order of reality. **"[The eternal Son] was born of the Father before all creatures; [but] after He had ministered to the Father in the creation of all things, . . .[35] He emptied Himself and was made man. Although He was God, He took flesh; and having been made man, He remained what He was, God. He took a body like our body, differing only in this, that it was born of a Virgin and the Holy Spirit."[36]**

If Origen did not actually coin the term *Theotokos* (and he may have), he certainly seems to have popularized it. The fifth-century historian Socrates Scholasticus tells us that Origen did not hesitate to use "Mother of God" in his long-lost *Commentary on Romans*—arguing that in Christ Jesus **"there are not two beings, but one single being"** —and **"gives a full explanation of why Mary is called** *Theotokos***".**[37] Dionysius of Alexandria, the most famous of

[35] Cf. Jn 1:1–3.

[36] *FEF* 1:191, no. 445.

[37] Socrates, *History of the Church*, 7:32 quoted in Gambero, *Mary and the Fathers of the Church*, pp. 73–74.

Origen's own disciples, used the word himself not long after this, its *second-earliest* appearance in Christian literature. **"Therefore, it is wise"**, Origen writes elsewhere, **"to accept the meaning of Scripture and not to pay attention to those who say that [Jesus] was born through Mary, not of her. The prescient apostle [Paul] has said: 'But when the fullness of time had come, God sent his Son, born of a woman, born under the law, to redeem those who were under the law'** (Gal 4:4). **Observe that he did not say: 'born *through* a woman', but rather, 'born *of* a woman'."**[38] This enthusiastic championing by Origen—who crowned his brilliant testimony with martyrdom—may be why we first see prayers like the one in the Rylands Library beginning to appear in his immediate wake.[39] Origen's great extra-biblical term *Theotokos*, at any rate, like that other indispensable term we

---

[38] Origen, *Commentary on the Letter to the Galatians*, quoted in Gambero, *Mary and the Fathers of the Church*, p. 73.

[39] To "pray" has acquired a uniquely God-ward orientation in English, but this is largely a trick of the language. One can still hear its original, more general usage in Shakespeare and the like; i.e., "I pray thee, sir", as a respectful form of request, and so forth. Spanish shows this better, where *oracion* means both to pray and simply to speak (even in English, we sometimes refer to a speech as an "oration"). Praying, then, to Mary is merely an old-fashioned way of saying one "speaks to her in a tone of respectful request". Origen himself adds this in his *On Prayer*: "Then, too, it is not foolish to offer supplication, intercession, and thanksgiving also to the saints. Moreover, two of them, I mean intercession and thanksgiving, may be addressed not only to the saints but also to other people, while supplication may be addressed only to the saints if someone is found to be a Paul or a Peter so as to help us by making us worthy of receiving the authority given them to forgive sins" (*On Prayer*, 14.6, in Origen, *An Exhortation to Martyrdom, Prayer, First Principles: Book IV, Prologue to the Commentary on the Song of Songs, Homily XXVII on Numbers*, trans. Rowan A. Greer [New York et al.: Paulist Press, 1979], pp. 111–12).

reviewed, was finally sanctioned officially at one of the great ecumenical councils (the First Council of Ephesus in 431), just as the Trinity had been at First Nicaea (325).

Eighth Circuit struck down

Jazz Theology

More than 130 years after Origen's death, a scholarly monk named Rufinus decided to create a new translation of the author's most famous book *De Principiis*, ("The Fundamental Doctrines"), in response to a recent spate of harshly negative criticism it had begun to receive from certain quarters. Rufinus, like most other Christians of the fourth and fifth centuries,[40] looked on Origen as a heroic, near-legendary figure from the Church's colorful past; and he seems, along with his schoolmate Jerome, to have been a "fan" from his youth. Now about fifty years old, Rufinus likely looked on the new wave of disparagement—from writers like Methodius and Epiphanius—as fashionable revisionism, a fad needing his own help to pass quickly. So Rufinus undertook the project with great gusto, looking forward to getting back into Origen again after a hiatus of some years.

Those 130 years had, by the way, been nothing less than *earth-shattering*, whether looked at in Christian or in secular terms. They had seen the worst and final wave of persecu-

---

[40] Athanasius, hero of the Arian crisis, praises Origen many times. Prierius, one of Origen's successors at the head of the Catechetical School was so in debt to him that Jerome calls him "Origenes, Jr." Jerome also opines that Eusebius of Vercelli, Hilary of Poitiers, Ambrose of Milan, and Victorinus of Pettau were all virtual plagiarists of Origen. Sts. Basil the Great and Gregory Nazianzen collaborated on an anthology of his writings, and their friend and collaborator Gregory of Nyssa called Origen "the prince of Christian learning".

tion—that of Diocletian in 303—give way suddenly to the
legalization of Christianity by the dying Galerius; the end,
at last, of Hermas' great tribulation. They had witnessed
a few years later the once-unthinkable conversion of the
Roman emperor himself, Constantine the Great; followed
shortly by the Council of Nicaea and the calamitous Arian
crisis that came in its wake, still the closest the Catholic
Church has ever come to defaulting on her faith outright; a
period when, by sober accounting, at least eight out of ten
Christian bishoprics had fallen into the hands of christo-
logical heretics, deniers of the full divinity of our Lord Jesus
Christ. Then, the evil spell had been broken by the arrival of
the much-dreaded "anti-Constantine" Julian the Apostate,
for fear of whom all the cowardly Arian accommodations
had been undertaken to begin with. Julian's sudden death in
battle on June 26, 363, had allowed a new line of Christian
emperors to arise, culminating in the accession of Theodo-
sius, who, with his Edict of Thessalonica in 380, first made
orthodox Christianity the official religion of Rome.

Now, as Rufinus began his translating in 394, the Church
was slowly recovering her health . . . but still suffering, it
seems, from a collective case of PTSD. For a man who had
lived to see one iota's worth of difference in a single theological term (*homoousios* vs. *homoiousios*)[41] cause a Christian-on-
Christian persecution as violent as anything Nero or Severus
ever dreamed up, Rufinus' first reentry into Origen's free-
wheeling world of openness and allegory must have been

[41] The Arians had added that single Greek letter into the Nicene word
meaning Christ is "of one substance" with His Father in order to alter it
into "of a similar substance"—their clever dodge to evade actual orthodoxy. This difference seemed so miniscule to later generations that scoffers
like Tom Paine were still mocking it 1300 years later.

like a dive from the rocks into a frigid mountain stream. Rufinus himself, it seems, had not quite remembered his hero's writings containing so many things that looked, in retrospect, to be, well, a little crazy. Taken out of his original context, Origen—whose name had once been "so highly esteemed that when there was a question of putting an end to a schism or rooting out a heresy, appeal was made to it"[42] —appeared actually shocking. The Church had, to say the least, learned to parse her words a good deal more carefully since then.

Origen's literary output really had been insane. From the time he took over the Catechetical School to his death at age sixty-nine, he composed at least two thousand individual works (Epiphanius has it at six thousand!), and many scholars rate him as the single most prolific writer of antiquity. These numbers are easier to credit when we realize how the miracle was accomplished. One of his admirers, a well-to-do merchant named Ambrose[43] whom Origen had reclaimed for the Church out of a Marcionistic heresy, so hung on his every word that he paid a team of stenographers to follow him around all day! **"At least seven shorthand reporters worked in shifts and transcribed his dictation,"** according to Eusebius, **"and there were the same number of copyists and girls who were professional engrossers."**[44] Most of these thousands of books, then, cannot have been much more than transcriptions of the Great Man's stream-of-consciousness talk; but that talk must gen-

---

[42] "Article "Origen", in *CE*.

[43] Not to be confused with St. Ambrose of Milan, who lived a century later.

[44] Eusebius, *Church History*, bk. 6, chap. 23, as quoted in Mike Aquilina, *Villains of the Early Church* (Steubenville, Ohio: Emmaus Road, 2018).

uinely have been worth remembering, given the exalted reputation Origen won during those years. His approach to biblical scholarship appears to have been equally unstructured. Though Origen carefully compiled his own unique edition of the Old Testament in which six surviving manuscripts —all somewhat different, some longer, some shorter—ran side-by-side on the page for ease of comparison, he seems to have exerted little effort to determine which of the six might be closest to the original autographs. **"Since he did not know the authors, he simply stated that he had found this one in Nicopolis near Actium and that one in some other place."**[45] He appears to have collected them, in other words, out of his sheer appetite for the Word of God, looking happily upon all the "extra" material as just more grist for the mill![46]

Origen's interpretations of Scripture were all over the map, as well: "he gave", as commentator Mike Aquilina puts it, "many interpretations of Old Testament stories— sometimes different interpretations of the same story. This was not a fault in Origen's view: for him, the same story could have many interpretations. The Exodus was an event in history, but it could also be the passage from error to truth or the passage from this world to the next. All three interpretations, and more besides, could be true at the same time. So there's a certain improvisational quality to some of

---

[45] Ibid., chap. 16.

[46] The Jews held at least three distinct groups of Old Testament manuscripts in Origen's day, all containing significant differences, and had only recently begun to favor exclusively what we now refer to as the Masoretic text. Christians, meantime, continued to prefer the Septuagint translation and the underlying texts (now mostly lost—though some were found among the Dead Sea Scrolls) that formed the basis of it.

Origen's Old Testament interpretations, and even his New Testament interpretations." Call it *jazz theology*—Origen riffing joyously off his own previous work, over and over in ever-widening circles of profundity, like Charlie Parker's endless arpeggios.

Now, however, the very peace of the Roman Empire hung on careful theology, and the science had grown correspondingly "uptight" as a result. In this new context, Origen's innocent frolics in the scriptural fields of the Lord appeared irresponsible in the extreme. Rufinus' rereading of *De Principiis* revealed one dodgy bit of Platonic speculation after another. Origen guessed, for instance, that Satan—who had, like Adam, fallen through his own free choice—might one day be saved like Adam. He wondered to what degree the *imago Dei*—the Image of God—had been lost in man at the time of Adam's fall and whether Adam and Eve might have existed as beings of pure spirit before that time. This, in turn, led to a practical denial of the resurrection of the flesh, his belief that death would free believers from all the material shackles they had gained purely as a result of Adam's sin. At one point, Origen ventured the opinion that human souls must have some kind of preexistence before conception— as God the Son had existed from eternity prior to his own conception in the womb of Mary. Origen even conjectured that the omnipotence of God might not rest until every single human soul had been conquered by mercy, and even hell itself might prove in the end to have been only a refiner's fire. Worst of all, his inadequate explanations of the Trinity now smacked of the later Arian enormities—though, with the 20/20 vision of hindsight, the same impression might easily be gained from a cynical rereading of Justin or Irenaeus as well.

Only the last of these notions, the defect in Christology now known technically as *subordinationism*,[47] had ever been officially anathematized by the Church—and that ruling happened *seventy-two years after* Origen's passing. None of the other oddities had yet been addressed by Church authority, nor were any of them explicitly contradicted by any single passage of Scripture. Rufinus, nevertheless, now knew why Origen's latter-day critics were raising such a fuss. Indeed, the remainder of the Man of Steel's personal history suddenly made more sense in this light. Demetrius, his bishop at Alexandria, the very man who had installed him as headmaster of the School there, became angry in 219 when Origen, a mere layman, was allowed to teach bishops during an extended stay in Palestine. When, fifteen years later, two of those same bishops ordained Origen themselves in order to nullify Demetrius' cause for objection (something Demetrius himself had been mysteriously chary about doing), the Egyptian prelate violently overreacted (at least in the eyes of Rufinus) by excommunicating Origen and banishing him from Alexandria.[48] Our hero taught the rest of his career from a new school at Caesarea in Palestine. Rufinus now wondered, it would appear, whether Origen's

---

[47] Subordinationism asserts that the Son and the Holy Spirit are, in nature and in being, subordinate to God the Father rather than eternally co-equal with Him, as in orthodox theology. St. John Henry Newman denies that Origen ever actually held subordinationist beliefs: "After his death, Arian interpolations appear to have been made in some of his works now lost, upon which the subsequent Catholic testimony of his heterodoxy is grounded . . . [while there is no doubt] that in his extant works, the doctrine of the Trinity is cleanly avowed": John Henry Newman, *The Arians of the Fourth Century*, 3d ed. (London: Lumley, 1871), p. 101.

[48] "St. Jerome declares expressly that he was not condemned on a point of doctrine": article "Origen", in *CE*.

eccentricities had been looked at askance even in his own day. Perhaps his doubtful contemporaries had picked away at his various canonical irregularities (the illicit ordination and his long-ago castration) in lieu of attacking his ideas directly—for fear of getting the short end publicly in a debate with the greatest mind of the age.

Rufinus, at any rate, now took an ill-advised step that backfired on him badly—and, indeed, on the whole Church. He went ahead with his translation project, but appears to have deliberately *toned down* the troublesome passages; so thoroughly, in fact, as to border on out-and-out falsification. Or so said his old friend Jerome, anyhow. Despite the fact that they had both been great admirers in the past, Jerome had now begun to side publicly with Origen's critics —and was thus especially stung by the fact that Rufinus' new translation opened with an old quote from Jerome himself, full of gushing praise for Origen! "This allusion annoyed Jerome, who was exceedingly sensitive as to his reputation for orthodoxy, and the consequence was a bitter pamphlet war, with Rufinus' *Against Jerome* and Jerome's *Against Rufinus*."[49] Eventually, Jerome produced his own, more literal translation of the passages in question, "but probably not less biased, as it was designed to show Origen's heresies at their worst."[50]

And this is pretty much how the controversy continued

---

[49] Article "Tyrannius Rufinus", *Wikipedia*: wikipedia.org/wiki/Tyrannius _Rufinus. Ironically, "St. Jerome is perhaps the Latin writer who is most indebted to Origen. Before the Origenist controversies he willingly admitted this, and even afterwards, he did not entirely repudiate it." "Origen", *CE*: www.newadvent.org/cathen/11306b.htm.

[50] *FEF* 1:190, Introduction to Origen.

from then on: both sides talking past each other, pep-
pering their charges with personal insults, and overstat-
ing their respective cases. This is also how, ultimately, Origenes Adamantius, "scholar of the early Church, a man of
spotless character, encyclopaedic learning, and one of the
most original thinkers the world has ever seen",[51] wound up
on the Church's bad side, or, at least, on her "watch list",
where he remains today. Twice more over the next two
centuries, Origen's name came to be linked to a whole class
of errors he himself never actually made, as "Origenism"
became a loose catch-all for any theological mistake made
through excessive allegorism or too heavy reliance on Greek
philosophical concepts. Theophilus, irascible Patriarch of
Alexandria during the early 400s, made a great show of condemning Origen's memory based on the objections raised
by Jerome—then used that condemnation to attack other
Origen "fans" such as St. Isidore (who had recently called
Theophilus out for financial irregularities at his church) and
St. John Chrysostom, whom Theophilus envied for his great
influence and popularity. This fight resulted, in the end, in
a synod held at Constantinople at which "Origenism" was
condemned; and then, in a paschal letter from Pope Anastasius I (399–401) repudiating Origen himself. Another ker-
fuffle, equally edifying, broke out in 543, at the conclusion
of which Pope Vigilius and all the Eastern patriarchs pro-
nounced fifteen anathemas on Origen's doctrines and afterward expressed their sincere wish that his name would
quickly be forgotten forever.

---

[51] Johannes Quasten, *Patrology* (Allen, Tex.: Christian Classics, 1986),
2:37.

That, obviously, has not exactly happened—but then neither has Origen's name been canonized, despite his martyrdom under Decius. That martyrdom, by the way, had taken
place in 263, but only after **"the demon of evil marshaled
all his forces, and fought against the man with his utmost
craft and power, assaulting him beyond all others against
whom he contended at that time."** Eusebius describes **"how
many things he endured for the word of Christ, bonds
and bodily tortures and torments under the iron collar
and in the dungeon; and how for many days with his feet
stretched four spaces in the stocks he bore patiently the
threats of fire and whatever other things were inflicted
by his enemies"**—and also tells **"what words he left after
these things, full of comfort to those needing aid"**.[52] As it
happens, Origen did not actually die during this horrifying
imprisonment. His judge seems to have released him, for
whatever reason, so that he lingered on, suffering greatly
from his wounds, for another two years or more. "He was
buried", according the Catholic Encyclopedia, "with honour as a confessor of the Faith. For a long time his sep-
ulchre, behind the high-altar of the cathedral of Tyr, was
visited by pilgrims. Today, as nothing remains of this cathedral except a mass of ruins, the exact location of his tomb
is unknown."[53]

The Teaching Church

So, was Origen a heretic—and if not, why not? Were
Theophilus and Anastasius right to condemn his work? And

---

[52] Eusebius, *Church History*, bk. 6, chap. 39.
[53] Article on "Origen", in *CE*.

if so, what does that mean for the idea that these Church Fathers act as a good guide to pure, early Christian doctrine?

Let us address those first two questions first. We can start by establishing the facts of the case a bit more clearly.

To begin with, none of us today is quite sure *what* Origen actually wrote; the later hysteria surrounding "Origenism" left us quite a mess. According to Newman, "his writings were incorrectly transcribed even in his lifetime, according to his own testimony"[54] and *De Principiis*, the book that stirred up most of the controversy, now exists only in the form (you guessed it) of Rufinus' doubtful Latin version. In the wake of Theophilus' ruling against Origen, the emperor Justinian went on one of the saddest rampages in the history of Christian literature; he was determined, as Mike Aquilina writes, "to root out all heresy from his territory. Justinian was not a well-educated man, but he was enthusiastic. He had heard that Origen's works were heretical, so he had them systematically rounded up and destroyed. We are lucky to have what we do have", a tiny fraction of his many hundreds of books. We are not even certain that Origen or even Origenism was actually anathematized by the pope. "Many learned writers believe so", according to the Catholic Encyclopedia, "[but] most modern authorities are either undecided or reply with reservations. . . . It may be held that the fifth general council was convoked exclusively to deal with [an unrelated affair] . . . neither Origen nor Origenism [was] the cause of it. . . . [But] an admitted Origenist, Theodore of Scythopolis, was forced to retract"

---

[54] Newman, *Arians of the Fourth Century*, p. 98.

some of his own errors there, "[so] it is easy to understand how this extra-conciliary sentence was mistaken at a later period for a decree of the actual ecumenical council."[55] Pope Anastasius' statement is actually very careful and limited; rather than condemning Origen and his work entirely, he condemned "everything written by Origen in the past that contradicts our faith".[56]

Even if Origen really is guilty, however, of every single doubtful stretch imputed to him (and it actually is best, I am afraid, as a matter of prudence, to treat him as guilty until proven innocent), another set of considerations is vitally important to factor in. This is Origen's own hesitancy in putting forth his theories and his constantly repeated willingness to have the officers of the Church sit in judgment over his work. The preface to *De Principiis* itself contains one of his boldest demurrers on the topic: **"The teaching of the Church has indeed been handed down through an order of succession from the Apostles, and remains in the Churches even to the present time. That alone is to be believed as the truth which is in no way at variance with ecclesiastical and apostolic tradition."**[57] He follows this up quickly with a short summary of the basics, quite similar to the later Nicene Creed. For Origen to affirm, then, that he himself believes his own theories and thinks they might turn out to be true is not really the same as asserting that those theories are part of the special set of truths "handed down through an order of succession from the Apostles". "It is generally stated", writes patristic scholar W. A. Jur-

---

[55] "Origen", in *CE*.

[56] Aquilina quotes in the paragraph are from *Villains of the Early Church*.

[57] *FEF* 1:190, no. 443.

gens, "that Origen's heresies are nowhere clearer than in his work *The Fundamental Doctrines*. Nevertheless, it should be noted that he is generally very careful to distinguish between Catholic doctrine and his own speculations, which latter he presents as no more than possibilities which would have to stand the test of acceptance or rejection in the teaching Church."[58]

Origen's work happened incredibly early in Church history—he wrote a thousand years before King John signed the Magna Carta at Runnymede. Many of the solutions he guessed at were aimed at problems the rest the Church had not even uncovered yet, much less defined or hedged around with dogma. He was, as Mike Aquilina continues, sailing in uncharted waters—dealing in areas which were still open for inquiry at the time. Yet "he was not a stubborn man and he was always willing to give up an opinion if the Church decided definitively against it." **"I bear the title of priest"**, Origen once wrote, **"and, as you see, I preach the word of God. But if I do anything contrary to the discipline of the Church or the rule laid down in the Gospels—if I give offence to you and the Church—then I hope the whole Church will unite with one consent and cast me off."[59]** "A man animated with such sentiments may have made mistakes, because he is human," concludes French Origen scholar Ferdinand Prat, "but his disposition of mind is essentially Catholic and he does not deserve to be ranked among the promoters of heresy."[60]

---

[58] Ibid., introduction to Origen.

[59] Quoted in J. Daniélou, *Origen* (1955; Eugene, Ore.: Wipf and Stock, 2016), p. 8; Origen, *De Principiis*, 1.6.3.

[60] Article "Origen", in *CE*.

Yet Origen certainly does say things that do not now reflect the mind of the Catholic Church—as do many of the
other Fathers, as we have already seen. What, then, are we
to make of declarations such as that of John Wesley, for
instance, speaking from within the Anglican tradition (but
expressing the common Catholic or Orthodox belief)?[61]
"The Rule of Faith is delivered to us in the oracles of God
[the Scriptures], *and* in the writings of the ancient Fathers
of the Christian Church. May we be followers of them in all
things as they were of Christ!"[62] When Reverend Wesley
says "in all things", does he mean to assert that each and
every one of the early Fathers was personally infallible and
that we must follow them even into their personal quirks
and pet opinions? Of course not—as his own writings at-
test. All of our witnesses offer their private theories at times,
some of them more valuable than others, just like any other
set of men. It is when they all say *the same thing*[63] that their
works truly begin to *teach*.

And here is where we come back around to the quote with
which we began this journey, two books ago now: "The Fathers are primarily to be considered as *witnesses*, not as *authorities*. They are witnesses of an existing state of things,
and their treatises are, as it were, *histories*—teaching us, in

---

[61] Wesley's Anglicanism—along with that of his famous brother Charles
—remained very "high" or Catholic until the end of his life, so much so
that he was often accused of being secretly a Papist by his many enemies.

[62] Cited in *John Wesley in Company with High Churchmen* (London: Church
Press, 1870), pp. 2, 24.

[63] Cf. 1 Cor 1:10 KJV—"Now I beseech you, brethren, by the name of
our Lord Jesus Christ, that ye all speak the same thing, and that there be
no divisions among you; but that ye be perfectly joined together in the
same mind and in the same judgment."

the first instance, matters of fact, not of opinion. Whatever they themselves might be, whether deeply or poorly taught in Christian faith and love, they speak, not their own thoughts, but the received views of their respective ages." This passage from St. John Henry Newman comes from a sermon he preached while still installed as the Anglican vicar of the University Church of St. Mary the Virgin at Oxford. It seems appropriate to reference that message more fully now; not only as an aid for understanding Origen—in both his strengths and his missteps—but also as a fitting finale to our whole inquiry in these pages. No one, perhaps, has ever explained God's role for the Fathers more clearly.

The canon of Scripture was largely settled by the mid-sixth century, and the great scholars of that era had signed off on the work. Supposing someone were to inquire "how we know that Ambrose, Leo, or Gregory was right,"[64] asks Newman, "and our Church right, in receiving St. Paul's Epistles", for instance. "What answer should we make? The answer would be, that it is a matter of history that the Apostle wrote those letters which are ascribed to him. And what is meant by its being a matter of history? why, that it has ever been so believed, so declared, so recorded, so acted on, from the first down to this day; that there is no assignable point of time when it was not believed, no assignable point at which the belief was introduced; that the records of past ages fade away and vanish *in* the belief; that in proportion as past ages speak at all, they speak in one way, and only

---

[64] St. Ambrose was the late-fourth-century mentor of St. Augustine; Sts. Leo and Gregory were fifth- and sixth-century popes who both took a role in promulgating the decisions of the Synod of 397, where Augustine's canon was accepted and finalized.

fail to bear a witness, when they fail to have a voice. What stronger testimony can we have of a past fact?"

This is exactly the same kind of evidence we have, as Newman continues, "for the Catholic doctrines which Ambrose, Leo, or Gregory maintained; they have never and nowhere *not* been maintained; or in other words, wherever we know anything positive of ancient times and places, there we are told of these doctrines also. As far as the records of history extend, they include these doctrines as avowed always, everywhere, and by all." This is the measuring stick

> which saves us from the misery of having to find out the truth for ourselves from Scripture on our independent and private judgment. He who gave Scripture, also gave us the interpretation of Scripture; and He gave the one and the other gift in the same way, by the testimony of past ages, as matter of historical knowledge, or as it is sometimes called, by Tradition. We receive the Catholic doctrines as we receive the canon of Scripture, because, as our Article expresses it, *"of their authority"* there *"was never any doubt in the Church."*[65]
>
> And that they are Catholic, is a proof that they are Apostolic; they never could have been universally received in the Church, unless they had had their origin in the origin of the Church, unless they had been made the foundation of the Church by its founders. The Apostolic College [that original body of Twelve appointed by Christ Himself] is the only point in which all the lines converge, and from which they spring. Private traditions, wandering unconnected traditions, are of no authority, but permanent, recognised, public, definite, intelligible, multiplied, concordant testimonies

---

[65] Newman quotes here the sixth of the English church's Thirty-Nine Articles of religion.

to one and the same doctrine, bring with them an over-whelming evidence of apostolical origin. We ground the claims of orthodoxy on no powers of reasoning, however great, on the credit of no names, however imposing, but on an external fact, on an argument the same as that by which we prove the genuineness and authority of the four gospels. The unanimous tradition of all the churches to certain articles of faith is surely an irresistible evidence, more trustworthy by far than that of witnesses to certain facts in a court of law, by how much the testimony of a number is more cogent than the testimony of two or three. That this really is the ground on which the narrow line of orthodoxy was maintained in ancient times, is plain from an inspection of the writings of the very men who maintained it, Ambrose, Leo, and Gregory, or Athanasius and Hilary, and the rest, who set forth its Catholic character in more ways than it is possible here to instance or even explain.[66]

Origen is an indispensable part of this great chorus of tradition; even when he steps away from the consensus of his fellows, he warns us in advance and thus illustrates the principle of consensus at work.

And the grandest irony of them all? Origen himself is our ultimate proof of the Church's power to know her own mind—to grow without warping, to draw out fuller meanings without falsifying, to ingest new input (even from iffy sources) without poisoning herself. Despite his dazzling persuasiveness, in spite of his unquestionable sanctity, in the face of his unparalleled prestige during the era in which he lived, *the Church still weeded him out*—and may even, while doing so, have erred on the side of caution.

---

[66] John Henry Newman, *Historical Sketches: The Turks in Their Relation to Europe* (London: Longmans Green, 1920), pp. 380–82.

"I love . . . the name of Origen", Newman confessed in his autobiography. "I will not listen to the notion that so great a soul was lost; but I am quite sure that, in the contest between his doctrine and followers and the ecclesiastical power, his opponents were right, and he was wrong. Yet who can speak with patience of his enemy and the enemy of St. John Chrysostom, that Theophilus, bishop of Alexandria? who can admire or revere Pope Vigilius?"[67] That "man of strong heart," he concludes, the Man of Steel "who has paid for the unbridled freedom of his speculations on other subjects of theology, by the multitude of grievous and unfair charges which burden his name with posterity," disproves, "by the forcible argument of a life devoted to God's service . . . his alleged connexion with the cold disputatious spirit, and the unprincipled domineering ambition, which are the historical badges of the heretical party".[68]

His name may not be invoked at our Great Thanksgivings, but we may still, as a private practice, join the memory of Adamantius to those of Hermas, Clement, and Hippolytus when we cry out for the prayers of that "great cloud of witnesses" that has gone before.

"Another angel came and stood at the altar with a golden censer; and he was given much incense to mingle with the prayers of all the saints upon the golden altar before the throne; and the smoke of the incense rose with the prayers of the saints from the hand of the angel before God."—Revelation 8:3–4

---

[67] John Henry Newman, *Apologia pro Vita Sua* (London: Longmans Green, 1995), p. 23.

[68] Newman, *Arians of the Fourth Century*, p. 97.